ALMOST 13
Shaping your child's teenage years today

Other works by Claudia Arp include:
Ten Dates for Mates (1983)
Sanity in the Summertime (1981)

ALMOST 13

Shaping your child's teenage years today

CLAUDIA ARP

Thomas Nelson Publishers
Nashville • Camden • New York

Published in Nashville, Tennessee, by Thomas Nelson, Inc. and distributed in Canada by Lawson Falle, Ltd., Cambridge, Ontario.

Printed in the United States of America.

Unless otherwise noted scripture quotations in this publication are from THE NEW KING JAMES VERSION of the Bible. Copyright © 1979, 1980, 1982, Thomas Nelson, Inc.

The scripture quotation noted TLB is from *The Living Bible* (Wheaton, Ill.: Tyndale House Publishers, 1971) and is used by permission.

The excerpt from *How to be Your Own Selfish Pig* © 1982 Susan Schaeffer Macaulay is used by permission of David C. Cook Publishing Co.

The poem, "Love Letter from God," is used by permission of the poet, Tish Murphy.

Library of Congress Cataloging-in-Publication Data
Arp, Claudia.
  Almost 13.
  1. Youth--United States. 2. Adolescent psychology--United States. 3. Parenting--United States--Religious aspects--Christianity. I. Title. II. Title: Almost 13.
HQ796.A727   1986   305.2'35   85-29735
ISBN 0-8407-5493-0

ACKNOWLEDGMENTS

Thanks to Linda Dillow, my "adopted" sister and dear friend, for helping to get this book in process and all her encouragement and help along the way...

John and Jane Bell, Bill and Cathy Clarke, and Paul and Phyllis Stanley for their input into our families over the years and for being great role models for us to follow...

Cynthia Smith, a special friend, for her efforts and leadership in organizing the first few "Moms' Support Groups"...

All the moms in Moms' Support Groups for their feedback and help in making this book much broader than just a "one-family" experience...

Janet Thoma, my editor and friend, for her expertise and her nudge toward excellence...

Kristine Tomasik, for her creative help with the study guide which will enable moms to put this book into action.

To my team

Dave, my lover, friend, and "soul buddy" whose support, love, and encouragement kept me going...

Jarrett, Joel, and Jonathan...the three fantastic teens God has given me, whose willingness to share their lives and words lets you see a glimpse of "real life" at the Arps.

CONTENTS

PART ONE

The Need for the Four Rs of a Right Relationship

Chapter One

REMEMBER WHEN YOU HAD
ALL THE ANSWERS?

I'll never forget the summer I realized Dave and I didn't have all the answers for raising children. Coincidentally, or not so coincidentally, our oldest son, Jarrett, was thirteen and we were visiting the United States on home leave from our work in Vienna, Austria.

It had been a grueling couple of months. We had spent most of the time traveling from state to state seeing family, friends and those involved with us in our work in Austria.

Wanting the boys at least to enjoy two final weeks without the hassle of traveling from city to city, we arranged for our two youngest, Joel and Jonathan, to spend this time at Myrtle Beach with our good friends, the Bells. Jarrett stayed with my parents in a little town in north Georgia, Ellijay, and worked each day picking apples for my brother who is an apple grower.

Apple picking was an exhausting job for a thirteen year old who was not yet physically developed. Jarrett wore an apple pack, which became heavier and heavier as he dumped apples into it. Late each afternoon, when my parents asked him to go out to dinner or to accompany them on some other activity, he answered, "I'm so tired, I'd rather stay home."

Yes, he was tired, but he had an ulterior motive. That summer my parents had bought two new cars, a small beige Citation and a large tan Oldsmobile, and they left the keys in the ignition or on a kitchen shelf.

Jarrett was fascinated with the new cars, especially the Oldsmobile. In Austria, teenagers can't drive until they are eighteen, and he had already begun to complain about that. "After all, I could get a permit at fifteen if I were in the states," he often reminded us.

The temptation that summer was too great. Jarrett decided to teach himself to drive. When my parents went out and left him alone, Jarrett began his driving lesson in that shiny new Oldsmobile. First, he drove up and down their long asphalt driveway. Next, he drove into the field beside their house and circled around and around to practice turning the wheels. Finally, he got brave enough to drive on the hilly road in front of their home.

One day it was raining hard. Jarrett hit a slick spot on the road and lost control of the car. Skidding off the pavement, he crashed into a nearby bank. *Bam!* The front fender hit the rocky ledge. The car bounced off the rocks and spun around. *Bang!* The back fender bashed into the bank.

When my parents returned, Jarrett's explanation was, "Someone stole the car and drove it into the bank up the street."

My father went with Jarrett to the accident, but he didn't buy his grandson's story. Instead Grandfather questioned Jarrett until the truth came out, then he assured him, "Jarrett, we want you to know we love you. We forgive you." My dad knew Dave and I would be back in two days, and he wanted us to handle any punishment.

The minute we drove into the driveway I noticed that the tan Oldsmobile was gone. When Jarrett opened the door, I immediately asked him, "Where are your grandparents, Jarrett? Where is their car?"

"Ssshhh," he said to quiet me. "Joel will hear you. Be quiet. I'll tell you later. Everything's O.K. Believe me, Mom," he pleaded.

His quick answer didn't satisfy Dave or me, so I asked my parents. They also put me off. "We'll talk about it tomorrow," they said. I kept after all of them until Jarrett finally told Dave and me what happened.

That night I couldn't sleep. I kept asking myself, *Where did we go wrong? Should we have told my father to keep his keys in his pockets? After all, boys are fascinated by cars.* Finally I began to realize that Jarrett was getting to the age when we just couldn't lock up all the cars and other temptations in the world.

I tried to look at the positives. Jarrett was not hurt. Neither was anyone else. No criminal charges would be pressed. My parents had been loving and forgiving. In just a few days, we would be back in Vienna, and no one there would know what had happened.

But I could not forget the negatives. Where in the world would we get the $1,600 to fix my parents' car? Was this accident an indication of even worse things yet to come? How on earth would Dave and I make it all the way through the teen years of our three boys when there was already a major problem in the first year?

You may know how I felt. Maybe you are not facing a wrecked car, but you probably have your own version of the tan Oldsmobile story. Or if your child is still a preteen, you may not have faced a major problem yet but are already worried about the years ahead.

THE GOLDEN YEARS?

We all cringe when we hear statements like, "Better enjoy your children now. These are the golden years. They'll break your heart later!" The elementary years had their high times; planned summers and projects contributed to sanity but I wouldn't classify them as "golden," not with three active boys. From my perspective I wanted things to get better, not worse! How did I get into the motherhood bit anyway?

Don't misunderstand me; I had always wanted to be a mother. I'm the one who pushed for three kids instead of two, and I had always taken my job of mothering quite seriously. Definitely an overachiever as a mom, I had shelves of books on family and children to prove it. However it had not come easily for me. I had had to work hard because, growing up, I had never babysat and had never dealt with children. My worst memories from my kids' toddler years were the days when my friends and I babysat for one another to save money and all the kids were at my house.

The approach of adolescence caused me great apprehension, and I still remember my first feelings of panic when Jarrett began to make teenage noises at eleven and twelve. I had felt cheated because I had thought I still had months before he was to reach the teens. Or did I? The relative calmness of the elementary years had disappeared and all signs seemed to forecast turbulent times ahead. Were the teen years really terrible? Was there an outside chance they could be terrific? Not according to the opinions I had heard, and Jarrett's accident verified my worst fears.

The morning after Dave and I returned, we told Jarrett, "We'd like to take you to the Dairy Queen for a milkshake." Here, we felt, was a place for us to discuss the problem without the other boys overhearing our conversation.

At first we sat quietly and drank our milkshakes, then Dave began to talk about the accident. "When you were just a little guy, Jarrett, we could protect you. When you threw sand at a friend or threw rocks at cars, we could discipline you quickly and not much harm was done."

"But now the consequences are much, much greater. Another car could have been involved in the accident. The people in that car could have been hurt. You could have been hurt or crippled for life. You could have been killed." Dave paused to allow Jarrett to think about these possibilities. We both watched his eyes fill with tears.

Dave assured Jarrett, "We love you, son. Still we want you to realize the seriousness of this situation and future situations like it. You can be sure there will be other times when Mom and Dad are not around and you will be tempted. What are your standards? Are you going to stand firm, based on your own convictions?"

As I watched Dave and Jarrett discuss this, I felt that for the first time in his life, Jarrett was beginning to feel that he had to be responsible for his actions. He had been scared enough by the accident that he seemed to want to avoid another big mistake if possible.

Dave made it clear to Jarrett that we would pay the $1,600, but after he finished college he was to repay us.

After that discussion with Jarrett, Dave and I were faced with the question: Where do we go from here? We considered the way God forgives us, putting our sins as far away from Him as the east is from the west, remembering them no more.[1]

Jarrett had learned a big lesson, we felt. If we didn't put this mistake behind us, it could become a noose around his neck. If we continued to think, *We don't know if we can trust him,* he might begin to think of himself as a renegade. We decided to forget about the accident. The next day we took him with us to a speaking engagement in Atlanta and not once did we mention the tan Oldsmobile or the $1,600.

Help Needed!

However, Jarrett's accident led me to do some soul-searching: Did I have a good relationship with my children? How could it be improved?

Dave and I began to observe seemingly successful parents. What were their secrets? What were they doing right? We decided to come right out and ask them these questions, and we received a lot of good advice. As we sifted through the information, a few basics appeared, the bottom line being: It's the relationship that counts.

One couple challenged us, "Keep the relationship alive and growing. As long as you can relate and talk to each other, both you and your teen will make it through all the other problems that come along. You'll be too strict in some areas, and too lenient in others, but as long as you can talk about it you'll come out O.K."

Another couple added an important word of caution.

"Yes, the relationship is the key factor. But it's extremely hard to develop that relationship during the teen years if you haven't worked on it previously. Build a good relationship with your boys early. Do it now. Don't wait until later."

To make our relationship with the boys the top priority for the years ahead, what was needed, we felt, was a reasonable plan. Dr. James Dobson says it like this: "I believe we should give conscious thought to the reasonable, orderly transfer of freedom and responsibility so that we are preparing the child each year for that moment of full independence."[2]

When we set our annual and five-year goals that fall, we specified strengthening our relationship with the boys. For instance, one of Dave's goals was: "Take Jarrett out to breakfast once a month and discuss a specific chapter from the book *Dare to Be Different* by Fred Hartley." Each year after that we reevaluated the steps we had taken that year, discarded the ineffective ones, tried to strengthen the positive approaches, and looked for new ways to improve our relationship with our boys.

Friends began asking me, "How do you get along so well with your boys?" so I began sharing the ideas Dave and I had adopted. Soon women's groups were asking me to speak at their meetings and retreats. After a while the moms in my sessions began asking for something more than just one or two day sessions. "We need to stay involved with these principles each week," they said.

These pleas led me to form a Moms' Support Group in our hometown of Knoxville, Tennessee, in 1982, so mothers could get together weekly or monthly to encourage one another and apply the principles in this book. The next year, new groups were formed—some in other states, so I felt the groups needed a manual to use as a guide. That year I wrote the manual from which this book is taken.

All the Moms' Support Groups used this manual for their meetings. Members added their comments, their stories, and their ideas and suggestions to the ones I'd already written. They were glad to have these ideas included as long as their names were changed, so this has been done.

As you read this book, imagine that you and I and hundreds of other mothers are sitting in a room together discussing our preteens and teens. Some of the moms are almost through these years so their experiences tell us a lot about the times that lie ahead.

The suggestions and ideas of these moms and the opinions of experts in child development and child psychology, which are also included in this book, will help you prepare effectively for your child's adolescence. Now is the time to decide how you will guide your child through the teenage years, not later when you are faced with an emotional situation and unable to think clearly.

You, like the Arps and the hundreds of moms in the Moms' Support Groups, need a plan for getting through the years ahead. Your plan may not be the same as ours. My goal is not to give you a program, but to share with you some principles we've discovered, which are working for us, and to tell you that these years may actually be the best years of all! I call these principles the "four Rs": regroup, relate, release, and relax. The four Rs will lead you to develop a good relationship with your preteen, one which will last throughout the teen years and into your child's adulthood.

REGROUP

First you must be willing to look honestly at yourself, at your preteen, and at your relationship, because you cannot devise a plan for the teen years without first analyzing your current situation.

The paradoxical statement, "We change in order to remain the same," certainly applies to motherhood.

We constantly change the way we relate to our children over the years. During their babyhood we literally hand feed our offspring. We don't treat our eight year old the same as we do our toddler. But it all happens so gradually that we don't realize we are changing in order to remain the same loving, caring mother.

As the teen years approach, once again we need to change to remain the same. If we drag our feet or push too soon we can mar our relationship, so as we approach the adolescent years, it's time for us to regroup again and rewrite our job descriptions. At this stage of family life there is a real need for "planned" parenthood.

RELATE

Next you need to look at some of the major obstacles which block the relationship between you and your child. Most often these are issues that cause sparks to fly in your home: hours, hair style, homework. You need to ask yourself, "What areas are really important to me? How my preteen dresses? The music he or she listens to? Or his or her beliefs? The ability to withstand peer pressure? To stay away from drugs, from promiscuous sex?"

I'll tell you some real life stories and some principles to help you answer the important question: "What will be the major and the minor issues at our house?"

Finally, you'll need to ask yourself another question: "Do the major issues coincide with what I am saying to my children every day or am I nagging about the minors?"

RELEASE

Adolescence is, by definition, "the state or process of growing up." We need to prepare our teens to make their own decisions, which means gradually releasing decision-making power into their hands. By their senior year in high school, our teens need to be making their own decisions, so they can practice this process while they are still at home.

One dad commented, "The missing element with my kids was this: Starting at age thirteen I didn't communicate that we wanted to guide and develop them instead of control them."

Our challenge as parents is to learn to release our adolescents so they can graduate into adulthood. Two vehicles we have used in the Arp family are the Teenage Challenge and the Birthday Boxes of responsibilities and privileges. We'll talk about these ideas and many others in this section.

RELAX

It's hard to relax when you feel responsible for what you can't control. I like to remember the prayer used in Alcoholics Anonymous: "God, grant me the serenity to accept the things I cannot change, courage to change the things I can, and wisdom to know the difference."

One mom I know used to stare at that motto, which was written on the wall of the undercroft of her church. She knew it was true, but she didn't want to admit, "There are things in my life I can't control."

Finally, she realized that so many things in her life were out of control that she had to take the leap of faith. In this section, we'll be looking at just what we can influence and how to relax and trust God for what we can't control.

WILL I BENEFIT?

"Will this book really help me guide my preteen through the teenage years ahead?" you are probably wondering. My answer is a resounding "Yes!" Listen to the story of one of the moms who has used this material.

"Chuck was the kind of kid that could have gone either way," she admitted. "The year he was in the seventh grade I was paralyzed with fear. He had never been a very good student, but he had been a star football player. Then he was injured so badly he couldn't play for the rest of the season. His self-esteem was at an all-time low as he watched the games from the stands.

"Some of his friends were becoming fascinated with drugs. I could tell that for the first time he was being influenced by them. I was at my wit's end. Then I started coming to the Moms' Support Group.

"First I found support for me. I felt like such a failure and here were other mothers who were saying, 'My kid says he hates me, too!' I was also getting some help in understanding my son. I began to realize it was O.K. to overlook some of the negatives. His dress and slang vocabulary might not be what I would choose, but they weren't moral issues.

"I began to learn how to encourage Chuck and to let him know I was on his team. With football gone and no strokes for academics, I knew he needed something that he could do well. That spring I made a deal with him. 'You go out for track, and then you can play football next year.'

"Chuck discovered he was really good at the high jump. The more he practiced, the more he won. The more he won, the better he felt about himself. His grades began to pick up, and slowly he began to make a turnaround. By the end of the school year, we entered what we now refer to as the beginning of the 'up time.' Chuck was realizing he was an O.K. person in other people's eyes. I think my affirming him at home had a lot to do with how he perceived himself. His coach even commented, 'I've never seen such a dramatic change in a student in all of my years of coaching!'

"That summer we went to the lake, which got him away from the friends who were getting into drugs. I also encouraged him to swim competitively. By the end of the summer, he came in third in the city swim meet. My mom asked me why I was killing myself driving my kids everywhere. I told her, 'Mom, I'd rather drive than worry! If the kids are busy with track and swim meets, there's reason to say No when others want them to do questionable things.'

"Now Chuck is in the tenth grade. His grades still fluctuate up and down, but he's a changed person. It's amazing what can happen when you get your eyes off yourself and focus on how you can encourage your kid. The Moms' Group and the principles I learned there were a real lifesaver for me. It saved us from some bad, bad times, and you can quote me on that!"

This mom's story is typical of the experience of many other women in Moms' Support Groups. Maybe applying these principles will not produce such a dramatic change in your preteen, but then again, it just might!

If you are a mother of a preteen or elementary school student and if you are really serious about developing a relationship with your offspring that will weather the adolescent storms and last for a lifetime, then this book is for you.

PART TWO

Regroup: Evaluating Yourself, Your Preteen, Your Relationship

Chapter Two

WILL THE WELL-ROUNDED
TEENAGER PLEASE STAND UP?

"What happened to my little angel now that she has turned twelve? What once was a smooth, friendly mom-daughter relationship has turned into a volcano that is about to erupt at any time," one mother admitted in a Moms' Support Group.

"Fourteen was a fantastic year with Pete, but now that he's fifteen instead of maturing, he's regressed. Is there no hope?" another mother asked.

Perhaps you can identify with these moms. The trouble with figuring out what our teens are like is that by the time we do, they've done another flip-flop. The only thing that you can count on during adolescence is change!

CHANGING COLORS

One day soon after Jarrett became fourteen, he and I were talking in his room after school. I decided to ask him a question I had wondered about for many months, "Jarrett, how do you feel about life?"

He shrugged his shoulders as if he really didn't know or care, but finally he said, "Well, I'm not satisfied with my teachers, my friends, or the world situation."

This response sounded like typical teenage disillusionment to me, so I prodded a little more. "What about yourself as a person?" I asked.

Laughing, Jarrett said, "I'm the only thing that is perfect!"

I wasn't ready to let the subject be dismissed so flippantly. I really wanted to know how he was feeling. I wanted to understand him, so I waited a while and then asked, "How do you feel about being a teenager?"

Finally becoming serious, he said, "I really like it. I get to be an adult without all the responsibilities such as earning a living."

My reward for continuing this conversation had finally paid off! Sometimes our preteens and teens open up to us with no prodding; other times it's up to us to keep the conversation going.

By the time Jarrett was fourteen, he and I were learning to relate on a more adult level; yet although Jarrett was beginning to see himself in an adult role, this maturing teen also played cowboys and Indians with his younger brothers! Our problem as moms is how do we understand and accept a teen who changes like a chameleon, who puts on a different color every day? It was easier to accept the changes that normally occurred between babyhood and childhood. Even the "terrible twos" were at least predictable. It is tricky at best to try to understand our teens who are still in the process of trying to understand themselves!

FOUR TEEN PROFILES

Not only are our teens changeable, they are just plain different. If your kids are like ours, you may wonder how children growing up in the same environment, having the same parents and the same training, can be so different. Our Jarrett is so uptight and self-disciplined that he organizes the lives of everyone around him. Joel is so laid-back and relaxed that we wonder how he gets out of bed in the morning. Yet they have basically the same environment.

A few years ago at our house we decided to study our kids and their friends, and we came up with four teenage profiles, three of which are represented in our home. The names have been changed to protect, not the innocent, but me!

Maybe you'll find that some of the same teens live at your house. I have found that it helps to know what to expect and also to know that your teens are no worse than other adolescents.

Sally Sparkle

Sally is popular at school, very outgoing, and fun. If a party takes place, Sally's sure to be there or at least to have been invited. She adds that special spice to family life, but sometimes things can get a little too spicy! She has a permanent parking place by the telephone, and long telephone cords, which reach into the privacy of a bathroom, are just part of Sally's equipment.

She comes with a set of friends that always seem to be around. What a bore for Sal if she is forced to spend an evening alone. She is uninhibited and impulsive, a scary combination for moms! Like a butterfly she flits from one thing to another. Her good intentions are sincere but she is lacking in follow-through. As a result, Sally leaves a string of unfinished projects and many messes as she flits on to something new and more exciting.

At school Sally tries to keep her studies from interfering with her social life, so the teachers describe her as "playful," needing to concentrate more on her studies.

Take-charge Thomas

Tom, the organizer, is the leader in his group. You always know when Tom hits the door. He is the only teen who is disappointed when his biology teacher believes in creation; he was so well-prepared for a lively debate. Tom has enough self-confidence for the whole family. When questioned about his latest purchase and reminded that no one else is wearing such attire, he responds, "That's O.K., Mom, I set the styles!" Many times he is right!

Strong-willed and hard-working traits sometimes cause

him to be domineering and to walk over other people, especially his mom. He also tends to be selfish and relates to his world in light of Tom and his needs. He considers his brothers' and Dad's closets as his own and helps himself generously to whatever he needs. Patience and sympathy are definitely not his strongest attributes. His teachers enjoy his quick mind but could do without his sarcasm and "smart mouth," traits he developed at an early age. Without a doubt Tom is going to contribute to the world in one way or another.

Laid-back Larry

We all enjoy Larry's easygoing, calm disposition. His boiling point is so high he rarely gets angry, but watch out when he does because he's not always sure of the appropriate way to handle it. His listening ear and dry wit make him well accepted at home and with his peers, but he is much quieter than Tom and Sally. Once on a family vacation Larry was left at a pit stop in Reno and not missed by the family for the next fifty miles!

Life for Larry is a pleasant, unexciting experience. His biggest problem is that he is so s-l-o-w and unmotivated. He does not derive his sense of self-esteem from achieving in school work. "Larry's so pleasant to have in class," his teachers say, "but can you do anything to help me motivate him to work harder and faster?" He tends to be the underachiever but once his internal motivation clicks on, watch out! He has a steady consistency that we all can admire!

Roller-coaster Rene

Rene is our ultraresponsible teen. She's quieter than her brothers and sisters, but she has a rich inner life. While Sally Sparkle's feelings are oozing out on everyone, Rene's feelings are directed inward. She is really just as feeling-oriented as Sally and often rides her emotions like a roller coaster—high then low, up then down!

She is our deep thinker and creative teen. Sometimes she amazes us with her insights, but woe be to us when she begins to become negative and introspective. She is the one who tends to convince herself that she is unloved. Her teachers are quick to tell us that she is a good student, but they think she shouldn't take life so seriously.

WHAT'S YOUR COMBINATION?

No doubt you can already see some of these teenage characteristics in your preteen, so now's the time to take a good look at your child's personality. Dave and I found it helpful to consult a basic temperament chart (see illustration 1).[1] Obviously such a mechanical analysis does not allow for the many individual combinations, but it does help parents to identify the general characteristics of a particular child.

On this chart Sally Sparkle would have a sanguine temperament and Take-charge Thomas a choleric one. They are the two outgoing teens, while Larry (phlegmatic temperament) and Rene (melancholic temperament) are more introverted.

Where does your preteen fit? Probably he or she is a combination of two or three, perhaps 60 percent choleric and 40 percent sanguine or 70 percent sanguine and 30 percent phlegmatic. This is true in our family, but we have found that usually one temperament is dominant.

Our oldest son, Jarrett, is our Take-charge Thomas. He is determined and strong-willed, independent, courageous, and a leader. I remember the summer during the time we were international representatives for Campus Crusade for Christ in Austria. While we were visiting the United States on furlough, Jarrett decided that he needed army fatigues.

"But, Jarrett," I argued, "none of the kids in Vienna wear fatigues."

"That's O.K., Mom," he assured me. "I set the styles."

A few months after we returned to Austria, what was

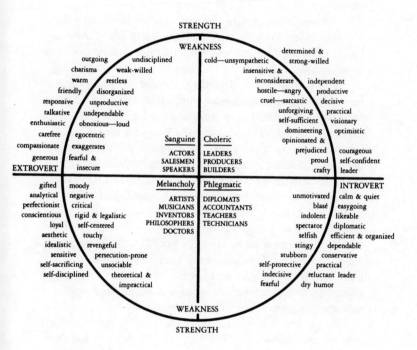

Illustration 1

everyone wearing on the next Boy Scout campout? You guessed it, U.S. Army fatigues!

Our middle son, Joel, is our Laid-back Larry. He is easygoing and likeable. When things get tense in our house, Joel will look around and ask, "Where is Humor?" His one-liners help to dispel a lot of tension.

Although he is bright, he generally finds school a drag. "I'd never want to make all As," he once said when Dave and I were discussing his grades with him. "It would be evidence of an unbalanced life!"

Our youngest son, Jonathan, is most like Roller-coaster Rene. He is gifted, analytical, and a perfectionist. He is the only Arp who would ever walk around for days calculating his math grade and be able to raise it from a D to a B in the last two weeks of a six-week grading period! We all need his quiet nudge toward excellence. I might add, however, that his perfectionism does not reach into all areas of his life.

Now that you've heard about our brood, look at illustration 1 and assess your preteen.

Remember Larry will never be as motivated as Tom, and Tom will never be as sensitive to others as Rene. Studying our preteens' temperaments encourages us to concentrate on their strengths and, at the same time, help them overcome their weaknesses. It also is an aid to helping us manage our own expectations as moms.

As parents we need to realize that each of these temperaments also comes with weaknesses. Sometimes we think about our kids as if they were characters in children's books like Little Lord Fauntleroy or Anne of Green Gables, who were perfect. The bad comes with the good, Mom. Looking at an assessment chart helps us realize it.

Now analyze yourself. After all, you're part of this equation. So is your husband. Merton and Irene Strommen (he is a noted research psychologist and she is a former public school teacher) said in their book, *Five Cries of Parents:* "Poor parenting can result from a parent's unresolved personal problems. There are brilliant psychiatrists and psychologists who know a great deal about the human personality, but are inept as parents. Their insecurities and needs, obvious to others but not to themselves, profoundly influence their actions. Though insightful and effective when helping others, they lose their effectiveness when dealing with issues that touch their own lives.... Having observed this phenomenon again and again, we find it crucial to encourage all parents to reflect on themselves as people and mates, as well as parents.[2]

Your temperament will affect how you relate to your preteen. A sanguine mom may try to act "too hip" or a choleric mom may try too much control. A melancholic mother may set too high standards or a phlegmatic mother may be too laid-back and permissive. Assess your own temperament. Be as alert to your own weaknesses as you were to your child's.

As I examined my own parenting and that of my friends, I noticed three different styles of mothering. Now that you have some idea of your personality, see if you recognize your parental profile. I've found some similarities between the way I nurture my plants, which is a favorite pastime of mine, and the way some of us parent our adolescents.

THREE PARENTAL PROFILES

The Smotherer

The smotherer wants to stay in control and help her preteen avoid mistakes that she made in her youth. Because of her fear, she shows a lack of trust and gives the impression that she is always trying to keep her child in the hot house, holding him or her back and pulling on the reins as the preteen surges ahead toward independence. The result of this method is a teen who resents and rejects parents and their ideas.

The Pusher

An equally disastrous approach is to push our children out of the home too soon before they are strong enough to survive on their own. The pusher expects her adolescent to become an adult overnight and gives freedom too quickly. The preteen does not have the maturity to make his or her own decisions and often becomes another peer pressure victim. Where is the balance between being a smotherer and a pusher? Consider one other option.

The Releaser

Young seedlings must be acclimatized gradually to the new environment in which they will grow by allowing them short times in the sun and wind with temperature variations in the real world outside the greenhouse. They must have a "hardening off" period. If the tender young plants aren't given this period to adjust, many will wither and die. However, if they are properly trained for survival in the new environment in which they are to grow, they will thrive, meeting your greatest expectations.

Our children also need a "hardening off" period, which gives them limited freedom and increased responsibility for themselves and their behavior under the watchful direction of their parents. We need to release them gradually. Our interaction with each other, which is greatly influenced by our different personalities, will provide a foundation for helping our teens enter the outside world.

APPLYING THIS KNOWLEDGE

Now that you have taken a critical look at your personality and your preteen's, think again about how you interact with one another.

I seem to be a choleric-melancholy personality. It's easy for me to try to control everyone and give orders. Hanging loose is foreign to my nature, so I have to watch being too uptight and trying to regiment the boys. On the plus side, I usually get our family moving when everyone else is in neutral. I also naturally encourage the boys.

How does my personality fit with the other personality types in our home? With each relationship, there is a different dynamic. Let's look briefly at a positive and a negative in my relationship with two of my boys.

Jarrett and I are naturally talkative so it's easy for us to be friends. However, Jarrett tends to be critical and I am sensitive, so he sometimes hurts me. We have to be willing to ask for forgiveness when we clash.

Relating to Joel is a different situation, since he is understanding and rarely critical of me. However, I have to watch asking too many questions, because Joel tunes me out if I do.

Now, think about your own family. How do your personalities fit together? Look at the Understanding Our Strengths and Weaknesses chart (exercise 1) at the end of the chapter. Think about your personality and your preteen's. How do you normally interact with each other? What are the potential positives? The negatives? What adjustments do you need to make to capitalize on the positives and minimize the negatives?

Unfortunately we cannot pick and choose our temperament or that of our adolescents. However we can modify our own, and we can observe and study each of our children. This will help us to understand and relate to them. Then we can be excited about the unique temperament God has given to each of us.

Think about how beautifully God created nature and how He cares about the blending of families. He did not make a mistake when He blended the personality types in our homes. When we begin to look at our unique preteens from God's perspective, we can appreciate and accept them just as they are.

Now is the time to take a moment to assess your preteen's strengths and weaknesses and plan what you can do to encourage the good and strengthen the weak areas. Fill in exercise 1, and refer to it every so often to see if you are following these plans.

UNDERSTANDING YOUR ADOLESCENT'S GOALS

Now that you've assessed your preteen's personality, let's consider some of a normal adolescent's goals. If you understand the desires that motivate your child's behavior, you will be better able to understand his or her actions.

In a recent adolescent-parent study which involved 8,165 young adolescents (grades five through nine) and their 10,467 parents, Merton and Irene Strommen identified seven goals, which most adolescents intuitively seek to achieve during the teen years:

1. Achievement—the satisfaction of arriving at excellence in some area of endeavor
2. Friends—the broadening of one's social base by having learned to make friends and maintain them
3. Feelings—the self-understanding gained through having learned to share one's feelings with another person
4. Identity—the sense of knowing "who I am," of being recognized as a significant person
5. Responsibility—the confidence of knowing "I can stand alone and make responsible decisions"
6. Maturity—transformation from a child into an adult
7. Sexuality—acceptance of responsibility for one's new role as a sexual being[3]

Those goals are no different from mine for my teen, you are probably thinking. However, friction develops when you and your child disagree about how to achieve these goals. For instance, motivated by a strong desire to broaden friendships, your teen may be overly susceptible to peer pressure.

Our goal as parents is to help our adolescents achieve these goals by learning to understand themselves and the world around them, rather than by grabbing at instant and compromising methods to fulfill these natural desires. The four Rs—regroup, relate, release, and relax—will help you to develop a logical plan to move your preteen along this road to adulthood.

THEY WILL NOT PASS THIS WAY AGAIN

The adolescent years are times of transition. Teens seem to have one foot in childhood and one foot in adulthood. They're at that uncertain, in-between age that at times can drive us moms up the wall. We aren't sure where they belong, and our teens don't know either.

When a friend's teen hit a hard place, the following advice was helpful: "Don't allow yourself to get frazzled about this stage because by the time you get into a total frenzy, she will have moved on to something else!" (Or if you want to think positively, it could be *something better!*)

Remember the best news is:

1. Each stage is progress.
2. Each stage is temporary.
3. Each stage is leading to adulthood.

Don't panic when your relationship appears to be breaking apart. Every once in a while, your preteen or teen may throw an "I hate you, Mom" in your direction. Usually, you will be friends again within twenty-four hours. Don't gloat and feel cocky, either, when your relationship with your preteen seems smooth. One mom I know wrote, "This is temporary!" and pasted it on her mirror.

Remember what Jarrett told me: "I get to be an adult without all the responsibilities." Allow your teen to be free to think as an adult and then to be free to play or react as a child at other moments. Remember teens are people in transition.

EXERCISE 1

Understanding Your Teen's Strengths and Weaknesses

I. Use the temperament chart to assess your teen's strengths and weaknesses and list them in the chart below.

TEEN ONE		TEEN TWO	
Strengths	Weaknesses	Strengths	Weaknesses

II. How can I help my teen to maximize his strengths?

III. How can I help my teen to strengthen his weak areas?

IV. A suggested prayer:
"Lord, thank you for _____ and for the uniqueness you gave to him (or her). Thank you for his (or her) strengths and help me to concentrate on them and to build him (or her) up in thse areas. Thank you too for his (or her) liabilities and help me to minimize his (or her) weaknesses. Show me how to help him (or her) in these weak areas without majoring on them."

Chapter Three

NO STRINGS ATTACHED

So you have a Laid-back Larry and a Roller-coaster Rene. You've seen their personality differences. You really want to relate. What's the next step? Understanding is vital, but we still need to clear the air and get on the preteens' team.

Often when we don't understand our preteens and teens, we think they are abnormal. We are scared because we can't relate to them. Because of our fear we try to change the adolescent, not by a revamp program jammed into one morning at breakfast, but by a subtle "reformation." What will happen? It might be something we don't like, so we've got to forestall the problem.

When the preteen was little, we saw things we didn't like: He or she was bossy or too lazy, too messy, or too loud. Over the years we worked on correcting these traits, but the child still exhibits bossiness or laziness and, coupled with adolescent ups and downs, these traits seem more glaring. We need to learn to accept our preteens unconditionally, as God accepts us.

One woman said, "I have worked hard on accepting my husband unconditionally but somehow never transferred this unconditional love to my teenage daughter. One day it hit me; it was as if God said, 'You're not applying all you know in this situation. You have your daughter on a performance basis—your love and acceptance is given *if* she tows the line, doesn't embarrass you, and is a shining example to friends, foes, and church members.' "

Probably we all can identify with this statement. It is hard enough to accept a husband who is an adult. How do you accept a teen who is paralyzed by peer pressure, who is

consumed with self, who is jubilant one day, in the pits the
next, a real teenage yo-yo? That is hard, so how do we do it?
First, we must understand God's love and acceptance of us.

GOD ACCEPTS US

The most wonderful thing that I have learned in my
forty plus years is that God loves me unconditionally. He
sent Jesus to die for me while I was still a sinner, not after I
had shaped up my life. He loves me, period, no strings attached, not *if* I am a perfect mom, and make all the right decisions. He loves and accepts me just as I am.

This total love has been the greatest motivational force
in my life. I want to become all that God wants me to be: the
woman, the wife, and the mother that He desires. This desire has not come from fear that God will reject me or be angry with me; instead it comes from thankfulness that He
accepts me as I am and sees me for what I can become.

This is what God wants us to do with our teens: to accept them as they are, in transition, hanging in the balance
between childhood and adulthood. These young people are
in search of who they are and how they fit; they are still under construction, developing physically, emotionally, intel-
lectually, and spiritually. When we accept them as they are,
then we can begin to encourage them to grow and become
all God wants them to become.

Here are three steps that will help you accept your
adolescent today. At our house we call this process "log removal."

STEP ONE: Remove the log.
The first step is to get rid of the negative. In Matthew
7:3-5, we read (in the Arp paraphrase):
"Why do you see the speck that is in your preteen's eye,
but do not notice the log that is in your own eye? Or how can
you say to your preteen, 'Let me take the speck out of your
eye' when there is the log in your own eye? You hypocrite,

How Do You Respond?

PRETEEN'S/TEEN'S FAULTS	WRONG RESPONSES	RIGHT RESPONSES
1. A smart mouth	I snap back, criticize, and give lecture no. 309.	Might say, "I realize you're upset with me, but how you're expressing it is unacceptable. Let's talk about it later."
2. Disrespectful looks	I jump on him— get hype, as he says.	Best to ignore. Later discusss nonverbal communication.
3. Seemingly uninterested in the Lord and spiritual things	I have a "pity party," and fail to see God's perspective. Look only at the now and not at what God might do in his life. I fail to remember that God cares more about his relationship with Him than I do.	Give some space. How you act is more important than what you say. Don't force-feed your preteen but try to expose him or her to Christians (see chapter 8).
4. Unkind to brothers	I become irritated, so I raise my voice and threaten punishment.	Don't raise voice. Say something like, "Hey, wait a minute, guys. In our family, we build each other up. There are enough people who will tear us down."
5. Demanding	I give too much and then am irritated and resentful.	Try a light statement like, "Sorry, I'm off duty."

Illustration 2

first take the log out of your own eye, and then you will see clearly to take the speck out of your preteen's eye."

We moms get so involved in seeing our preteens' ups and downs and in concentrating on all of their many faults that we cannot see our own faults.

Exercise 2 on page 50 is one Dave and I have used to help us get our eyes off our boys' faults and instead get the logs out of our own eyes. In the left-hand column, we listed our preteens' faults. We let our minds go wild and made a long list. Then in the right-hand column we wrote down our wrong responses to their faults, a much harder task than naming the faults. Perhaps your preteen or teen gave *messy* a whole new meaning. What is your response to his messiness? Do you nag, sigh, yell, compare him with other teens whose middle name is "neatness"? We also include as an example one mom's honest appraisal of her wrong responses to her preteen's faults and the right responses she should have made (illustration 2).

It's Your Turn

Stop right now and do Part I of exercise 2. You might turn back to exercise 1, where you listed your teen's weaknesses. Feel free to let your mind race and add to this earlier list. No matter how long this list becomes you may be surprised that your wrong responses are just as bad as your preteen's faults. After you have finished, confess your wrong attitudes to God. Do not show this page to your preteen! (You may want to photocopy the exercise, then fill it out.) This exercise is to help you get the log out of your own eye, to rid yourself of the negative, so you can begin to see the positive qualities in your preteen.

Now fill in the last column. Decide what your responses should have been. Once you've thought through the negative ways that you and your teen interact, you will be better able to stop yourself in the middle of one of these scenarios and plug in the right response.

STEP TWO: Be thankful for the positive qualities.

Does your preteen really try to perform well in school? Does he call you when he is going to be late? Is she trying to control her temper? Is she trying to be more cooperative? Thank God for these things! In Philippians 4:8, we read (again my paraphrase):

"Finally, mom, whatever is true about your preteen, whatever is honorable, whatever is just, whatever is pure, whatever is lovely, whatever is gracious, if there is any excellence, if there is anything worthy of praise in your preteen's life, think about these things."

It is a tragedy that too many of us moms have interpreted this verse to read:

"Finally mom, whatever is untrue, whatever is unhonorable, whatever is unjust, whatever is impure, whatever is unlovely, whatever is ungracious, if there is anything not excellent, if there is anything not worthy of praise in your preteen's life, think on these things."

Too often moms dwell on the negatives so all the preteen or teen hears are discouraging statements. One counselor commented: "So many times I see parents become tremendous flaw-pickers, pointing out all the shortcomings and faults of their teenagers. This kind of experience during those turbulent adolescent years can do nothing but drive the kid we love from our home and get him hooked into whatever is the vogue in the peer group."[1]

Think Positive, Mom

I challenge you to dwell on the positive qualities in your preteen or teen's life. I challenge you to become more positive, so your preteen or teen is encouraged and built up. Turn again to exercise 2 and make a list of all your preteen or teen's positive qualities. You'll be surprised at how many there are.

One word of caution: Don't do the one exercise without doing the other. You must look at both the good and the bad to see your preteen completely. After you make your list, keep it so you can refer to it on your "down days," like the one I had not too long ago.

Personally Applied

Dave and I had just finished leading three marriage workshops in six weeks, I had a terrible cold, and I was frantically trying to pull together a speech on "Relating to Those We Love" for a large women's conference. I was feeling lousy and inadequate. At noon that day I opened my mail and found the contract for this book. All of a sudden I realized how much nerve I had even to consider writing such a book. Were my kids perfect?

That afternoon I began watching Joel and Jonathan's every move. Joel was the first to fail this inspection. "Mom, my résumé for my Eagle Scout award needs to be in tomorrow. Would you help me with it?" he asked after he'd had his usual snack.

I was just beginning to get my speech outlined, but I put down the pen and answered, "O.K., let me see what you've done."

"Oh, I haven't done anything, yet," answered our laid-back teen.

"You haven't begun, and it's due tomorrow!" I gulped and decided it wouldn't do any good to lecture now. I'd been down that road before, and the fight that followed such a lecture just upset us both and wasted valuable time. "O.K., why don't you sit here at the table and write a list of everything you've done that shows dependability, skill, and leadership. When you're finished, we'll look at it together."

Twenty minutes went by. "Well, Joel, let me see what you have done," I said as I observed his half-empty page.

"Guess I'm just not that great!" he said with a chuckle.

Why can't Joel be motivated and serious? I thought. I'd learned to keep thoughts like this to myself, so I didn't say anything to him. Instead we worked together for the next hour, listing all his honors and accomplishments. Mom was definitely more interested in this project than son.

"Can I go now?" he finally asked.

With a mixture of relief and discouragement, I said, "O.K., but don't forget to type it before tomorrow." Once Joel was gone I looked over the résumé. It obviously needed a lot of editing and fine tuning. Our family sure needed that same kind of fine tuning. *I must be crazy to be writing this book,* I thought again.

A few minutes later, Jonathan walked into the kitchen. "You know, Joel really hates me," he said. "You should see the way he looked at me just now. Why don't you correct him once in a while? You're always correcting me! He doesn't deserve to be an Eagle Scout; they're supposed to be courteous and kind."

"My, Jonathan, where did you find that fabulous mood?" I inquired, hoping to laugh off his negative feelings. No such luck. He went into a discourse on the injustices he had suffered that day at school and ended with, "You'd feel the same way if you were me."

Jonathan had also failed the perfection checkout. I glanced at my unfinished speech. *Maybe tomorrow will be a better day,* I thought.

But breakfast the next morning was more rushed than usual. As Joel gulped down his last mouthful of cereal before racing outside to meet his ride, he announced, "I need a pencil."

"So do I," Jonathan chimed in. "And I'm going to beat you to it."

Both boys pushed back their chairs and raced to the

junk drawer where I kept a supply of pencils, which always seemed to disappear.

"See, I beat you, Joel," Jonathan shouted.

"I don't give a fart!" Joel snarled.

"Joel, that's enough!" I shouted. "I can't believe you would actually say something so vulgar. Guess you just don't give a fart about anything, do you?"

I broke into tears as they ran out the door to catch their ride to school. Why had I fallen into the same trap? Swearing and vulgar language are off-limits at our house. I had just flunked, too!

How could I talk to a group of women about relating to their families when I'd just blown that encounter? How could I sign a contract for the book *Almost 13* when my kids and I were far from perfect? Right now I wanted to kill my son, not love and encourage him.

Dave came into the kitchen and sat down for breakfast. He'd heard the commotion, and after one look at my face, he knew how I was feeling. After he made a few preliminary comments about the hassle, he asked, "Claudia, what advice would you give to a mom who asked what she should do in a situation like that?"

I shrugged my shoulders and gave him a that's-hitting-below-the-belt look. He didn't venture another comment until his usual, "See you tonight, sweetheart."

I sat at the kitchen table for the next twenty minutes. *What would I say to another mom?* Finally I asked God to quiet my anger and restore my perspective. *Show me how to get out of this mess,* I pleaded.

Remember Joel and I are completely different personalities. I sometimes interpret his easygoing attitude as indolence. When you mix my perfectionism and my tendency to try to control the situation with his personality, it's easy for us to clash.

What would I tell another mom? I wondered. I walked upstairs and got a copy of this manuscript and turned to this section. Slowly I reread my own paraphrase of Philippians 4:8: "Finally, mom, whatever is true about your preteen or teen, whatever is honorable, whatever is gracious..."

I'd tell that mom to make a list of her child's good qualities, I decided. That's just what I did. Let me share my list with you.

Joel's Positive Qualities
1. *He works on his grades.*
2. *He is finishing his Eagle Scout award.*
3. *He doesn't drink or take drugs.*
4. *He's responsible in his job.*
5. *He likes his home.*
6. *He gives me hugs.*
7. *He usually goes to church and Sunday school.*
8. *He likes his action group and Bible study group.*
9. *He goes to Student Venture, his youth group.*
10. *He's not into sex and girls.*

My list was longer than this, but you get the idea. I looked over the list and thought, *Gee, I'd like to have a son just like him.* My attitude and perspective were changing.

Next, I opened my Bible and read some of my favorite verses on hope, like First Corinthians 9:10, "...he who plows should plow in hope, and he who threshes in hope should be partaker of his hope," and Psalm 16:9, "My flesh also will rest in hope."

Then I called a friend to play a game of tennis. Physical activity always helps to relieve my frustration. Garden work is also excellent; I take my irritation out on the weeds and the crabgrass rather than my teen. All the time I was playing tennis I knew I would take the next step toward a good relationship with Joel: I'd ask his forgiveness.

STEP THREE: Ask for forgiveness.
In this section of the book, we are talking about relating to our preteens. Some of us, however, cannot relate

because we have been so negative in the past; our negative statements have blocked our communication. We have tried to change the preteens by nagging and have dwelt on the negative characteristics instead of the positive. Because of this, our kids think of us as someone who tears them down instead of someone who builds them up. Before you can relate to your preteen, you need to seek his forgiveness for your wrong attitudes. Do not do this hastily as an emotional gesture. Pray, ask God's wisdom, and meditate on the following verse (paraphrase mine):

"So if you are standing before the altar in the Temple offering a sacrifice to God, and suddenly remember that a preteen has something against you, leave your sacrifice there beside the altar and go and apologize and be reconciled to him, and then come and offer your sacrifice to God" (Matt. 5:23-24).

If after prayer and thought you feel the need to clean the slate and admit your wrong to your preteen, as I did, approach him in such a way that all the blame is cast on you. For instance, do not say, "Charlotte, because you have been such a hard person to live with and have been so moody, I have been negative too." Remember you are asking forgiveness, not criticizing her again.

Perhaps you could say something like this, "Charlotte, I've recently realized that I've been negative and not been an encouragement to you. I want to be different and ask you to forgive me. Will you forgive me?"

One mom in a Moms' Support Group found it difficult to ask her preteen's forgiveness so she wrote her a letter:

Dear Jennifer,

I hope you had a good day at school. I have spent a lot of time today thinking about our relationship. I realized how negative I have been lately and that you haven't heard much positive from me. I want to ask you to forgive me. We all have weaknesses, and I have been wrong to concentrate on yours when you have so many strengths. I am so thankful for you and want to be a more positive mom. Can we get back on the same team?

I love you,
Mom

Let's go back to my confrontation with Joel. When he came home from school that day, I apologized. I also explained why I had gotten so mad, so that he could understand my feelings. "I felt you were expressing your attitude toward your Eagle Scout award, toward me, and even toward God."

"Gee, Mom, I think you overreacted," Joel said.

I agreed with him. He was right and we both knew it. I've found that admitting my shortcomings to my kids helps them to understand me better; they even respect me more because I can admit I'm wrong. Realizing that parents are not always perfect also helps kids accept their own shortcomings.

Later that afternoon in Joel's room, we sat on his bed and talked and talked. "Mom, you should sign that contract," he said. "After all, you don't have to say any of us are perfect. Just that we try to do our best."

We talked about peer pressure and how important it was to Joel to know Christ and be committed to Christian values. In the middle of that conversation, he said one of those thank-yous that all parents cherish. "Mom, you and Dad have lived the values you've taught me. That's how I know they'll work."

Does log removal work? Emphatically yes. It's amazing how quickly communication can be restored when we parents deal with our mistakes and learn to ask our preteens' forgiveness.

EXERCISE 2

Accepting Your Preteen

I. Remove the log. (Matt. 7:3-5)

List:

My Preteen's Faults	My Wrong Response	My Right Response

II. Discern Positive Qualities

1.

2.

3.

4.

5.

III. Ask for forgiveness if needed (Matt. 5:23-24).

IV. Accept your preteen with no strings attached!

PART THREE

Relate: Eliminating Major Obstacles

Chapter Four

BIRD LEGS, BRACES, AND ZITS

Can you remember your junior high years? One mom found it helpful to recall how she felt when she was a pre-teen: "What horror fills my mind when I recall the beginning of my adolescent years! Skinny legs. Pimples. Perpetually imagining what others thought of me: Did they notice my crooked nose? My padded bra? The absence of a special guy to sit with at the Friday night football game? Why did I have to be a runt—small and skinny? And my eyebrows, why didn't God give me more? On top of all this—braces, too!"

"Inferiority" is the key word to describe these years; surveys show that up to 80 percent of young people do not like themselves. Many mothers I have talked to say that the age span from twelve to fifteen is the most difficult time in life. "We have the gray hairs to prove it!" they say. Self-doubt and feelings of inferiority reach an all-time high.

Dr. Urie Bronfenbrenner, eminent authority on child development at Cornell University, was asked during a United States Senate hearing to indicate the most critical years of a child's development. He knew that the senators expected him to emphasize the importance of the preschool experience, reflecting the popular notion that all significant learning takes place during the first six years of life. However, Bronfenbrenner said he had never been able to validate that assumption. Yes, the preschool years are vital, he said, but so is every other phase of childhood. In fact, he told the Senate committee that the junior high years are probably the most critical to the development of a child's mental health. During this period of self-doubt, the personality is often assaulted and damaged beyond repair.[1]

Many mothers with whom I have talked basically agree with Bronfenbrenner's statements, but they say girls often catch the inferiority disease before thirteen. I also know that some adolescents do exist who like everything about themselves. If you have such a preteen, rejoice!

Most of us would agree that the two most admired qualities today are beauty and brains. If you're a boy, you might add brawn. It's grossly unfair, but the intelligent, the attractive, the well-coordinated preteen seems to have a built-in advantage. Still that child may not realize it. I recently talked with a former Miss America who never saw herself as being especially attractive as she was growing up (yet she was a real beauty). Amazing as it seems, the beautiful, talented child also feels inferior.

How do you see your preteen? Is he or she a big hunk of potential? Or do you just see the deficiencies? Believe it or not, your preteen's image of himself or herself will probably match yours. Sometimes mothers have to believe in their children when the facts point another way. We have to accentuate the positive, eliminate the negative, and don't mess with Mr. In-between, as the old song goes.

I was raised in a family where grades and academic achievement were important. The two Cs I received in school were traumatic for me. I still remember the sinking feeling when Jarrett brought home his first report card. How could anyone make Cs in the first grade?

I bit my lip and took several deep breaths; then I gave him a hug and said, "Jarrett, this is a wonderful report card. You're passing everything! But there's also room for improvement. You have great potential."

At the time I didn't realize that this statement would be repeated year after year for the next nine years. Still I was convinced that Jarrett had great abilities, even when some of his teachers doubted it. Finally, during the last few years of high school, Jarrett realized that getting good grades was important to his getting into the college of his choice. The Cs were quickly replaced by Bs and a few As. Now that he is in college, he is excelling academically. Why? Jarrett thinks of himself as intelligent, just as I do.

He had a poster in his room during most of his teen years: "If you think you can or you think you can't, you're right!"

CONCENTRATE ON STRENGTHS

A teenager is like a jigsaw puzzle that is about three-fourths completed. Parents can see the framework, but they are so busy concentrating on the missing pieces, they don't appreciate the lovely developing picture.

I'm not saying ignore the holes and weak areas but do not concentrate on them. Admire the pieces that are there. The following letter written by a teen shows the devastation our negativism can bring.

Dear_____

I got one A, two Cs, and a D on my report card, which is great for a guy like me. My parents screamed their heads off about the D.

I built a pretty good model plane. All they saw is the mess in my room. I baby-sat my little brother the other day (for free). Instead of thanking me, they yelled because Larry broke the peanut jar. If I'd grabbed it instead of Larry, he would have fallen off the counter.

They tell me I'm clumsy, lazy, sloppy, and "can't you do anything right?" Then they lecture me on how I should change. I know I'm dumb and awkward. They don't have to rub it in. Sometimes I feel like I'm an eggshell—if I get one more knock, I'll crack.

About to Give Up[2]

Why is it that we concentrate on the missing parts of the puzzle? Could it be that our own insecurities as mothers are showing? If our teen is weak in an area, does this reflect on us and our training of him?

If your teen gets all As and Bs in school except for a C in French, what do you spend the most time talking about? Sure, he needs to work on French, but perhaps your student is just not great in languages. After all, as one teen told his mom, "You can know over half of the material and still get an F."

EVEN INFERIORITY CAN BE POSITIVE

Let's take a second look at the subject of inferiority. Sometimes a healthy sense of inferiority can be positive. You don't agree? You say, "I know what I'm talking about. I had a terrible inferiority complex when I was a kid."

So did I. Everyone feels inferior from time to time. Will Rogers once said, "I never met a man that couldn't do something better than me." A healthy sense of inferiority is knowing that there will always be someone smarter, prettier, more talented than I am. Too often we parents can accept our own inferiority, but we want our kids to be the best.

When we moved back to the States several years ago, our boys were experts in the European sports of snow skiing and soccer. They were some of the best skiers the Knoxville racing team had seen in a long time. They began collecting trophies. Before long, they were competing in the southeast division. You guessed it; here they met other teens who were just a little faster than they were. We had to help them realize that they weren't failures when they came in second or third or last, as long as they did their best and gave their all.

THE OTHER SIDE OF THE COIN

On the other hand, there are things each of us does well, often better than others. We need to identify the areas in which our children excel and help them capitalize on them. Be wary, however, of three pitfalls:

Pitfall One: We want our children to excel in our choices.

If Dad was a football star, he may push his son in this direction when Pete would rather collect butterflies. Look for your child's natural bent. Since Jarrett has always loved to argue and discuss ideas, I was not surprised when he was asked to join the college debate team. "You're a natural!" I told him. "You've been debating with me for eighteen years. I can't remember a time I won!"

Pitfall Two: We want our preteen to excel in everything.

The parable of "A Rabbit on the Swim Team" shows the fallacy of expecting your child to be good at everything.

Once upon a time, the animals decided they should do something meaningful to meet the problems of the new world. So they organized a school. They adopted an activity curriculum of running, climbing, swimming, and flying. To make it easier to administer the curriculum, all the animals took all the subjects.

The duck was excellent in swimming; in fact, better than his instructor. But he made only passing grades in flying, and was very poor in running. Since he was slow in running, he had to drop swimming and stay after school to practice running. This caused his web feet to be badly worn, so that he was only average in swimming. But average was quite acceptable, so nobody worried about that—except the duck. The rabbit started at the top of his class in running, but developed a nervous twitch in his leg muscles because of so much make-up work in swimming.

The squirrel was excellent in climbing, but he encountered constant frustration in flying class because his teacher made him start from the ground up instead of from the treetop down. He developed "charlie horses" from overexertion, and so only got a C in climbing and a D in running.[3]

Whether your preteen is a rabbit, a squirrel, or another unique "animal," concentrate on developing his or her particular talent.

Pitfall Three: We push our children too soon.

When we moved back to the States, we were appalled to see organized sports for four and five year olds and tennis lessons for toddlers. Sometimes we are so anxious for our children to succeed, we push them too fast.

If children do everything by the time they are ten years old, what will be left for the adolescent years? Now is a good time to stop and evaluate your child's activities. Does your preteen's irritability come from constantly practicing to be a prima ballerina when she should be enjoying her friends?

As long as you resist these pitfalls, you will be able to encourage your preteen to develop his or her talents. Then you need to let your child know you're on his team. Regardless of how your preteen feels about himself today (his feelings may change by tomorrow), he desperately needs your positive support. Let's look at some ways you can be an encourager.

FOUR TO ONE FOR ENCOURAGEMENT

Do you realize it takes four positive statements to counteract one negative comment? For the next twenty-four hours keep track of the number of positive and negative statements you make to your preteen. Too often the ratio of a parent's positive to negative statements is one positive statement to four negatives, instead of the opposite. And remember four positives to one negative is just staying even!

"Parents need to emphasize the positive—to confirm the things the kid does well, and for the most part, ignore the things he does poorly," said Jay Kesler, long-time president of Youth for Christ, in his book *Parents and Teenagers.* "It is far better to put the accent on the positive rather than to bandage up the negative. Ridicule always hurts, but a young person who is affirmed at home is in a good position to learn how to handle it."[4]

If we do not build up our preteens, who will? His or her friends? Probably not, since their favorite way of speaking is with cleverness and sarcasm, like the "cute quips" written in a teen's school yearbook: "To the useless hunk of junk!" "To the weirdo." "To the girl with the incredible hulk nose." "To bird-legs Bonnie."

Who will praise him? His teachers? Yes, some teachers do encourage, build up, and praise their students, but there are also those who teach by criticizing. Have you ever heard these comments? "Can't you do better than that?" "Are you stupid?" "Your writing looks like a five year old's." "I've given up on you." "Where are your brains today, in cold storage?" "How do your parents put up with you?"

Let's face it, we are the ones who care, who can love a sometimes unlovable, often irrational preteen or teen. We have the potential to be one of the most positive reinforcing agents in our child's life.

Be an Encourager

What comes to your mind when you think of praise? Is it a visit to grandmother's house as a child and hearing her tell you, "Honey, you're just the best little girl in all the world! You are so good"?

Ouch! That hurts! Why? You may not have been the resident rebel but the descriptive words *best* and *good* didn't exactly fit either. Too often when we think of praise, we automatically think of flattery and insincerity. This is not true praise. Let me share with you a few principles from the Arp definition of encouragement.

Encouragement is sincere. Flattery is insincere while encouragement and praise are sincere, positive evaluations of a person or activity. If you tell your preteen daughter that she is the prettiest girl in her class the same week she ate too much chocolate and has a zit to prove it, she will know you are insincere. Furthermore she won't believe you when you offer a real compliment. Keep praise sincere.

Praise is affirming what your teen is becoming. Goethe, the great German philosopher, said, "If you treat a man as he is, he will stay as he is, but if you treat him as if he were what he ought to be and could be, he will become that bigger and better man."

How does this relate to preteens? When your preteen shows real maturity or good judgment, slip in compliments such as these:

• "I really look forward to your being able to drive. I believe you will be an excellent driver."
• "You are going to make a wonderful wife someday, you are so caring and sensitive to other's needs."
• "It's rewarding to be your mom, but I also appreciate the friendship that is developing."

Do not forget to affirm your preteen in front of others, too, but be sensitive not to embarrass him or her.

Encouragement must be verbal. We can have all kinds of nice thoughts about our teen but their power is not released until we verbalize them. How much praise power have you released today? In the previous chapter we discussed Philippians 4:8 and the importance of concentrating on the positive. Now is the time to apply this principle. What can we as mothers do to combat the tendency to dwell on the negative? Here are two suggestions:

1. Memorize Philippians 4:8 and ask God to help you dwell on the fine things in your teen's life.

2. Then commit yourself to make praise a habit.

Remember that research reveals it takes approximately three weeks to develop a new habit and six weeks to feel good about it. A grumbler doesn't become an encourager overnight. But the good news is that psychologists David and Vera Mace say that it is possible to change and modify our behavior up until the day we die!

Begin by Beginning

A group of mothers was studying how to praise their families better and they sadly admitted that they lacked the habit of encouraging their teens. They committed to God and to each other to make praise a habit and began by praising their children five times the first week. One mom at the end of the first week said, "It felt so strange to hear the words of encouragement and praise come out of my lips."

It may seem strange at first, but let's do it anyway. Praise needs to become a daily verbal habit. It also needs to become a frequent nonverbal form of communication. Encouragement can be relayed in many ways. Following are some of the ideas we have tried in our home.

Thanksgiving Acrostic

One Thanksgiving I made a special acrostic plaque for each of our boys to express all the positive qualities I was thankful for in their lives. I used colored construction paper, pressed on letters to make the acrostic, and then mounted each of my creations in an inexpensive frame from the local discount store. The total time to make three framed acrostics was one hour. The Arp guys genuinely liked them and even hung them on the walls of their rooms alongside their posters, sports awards, and other treasures. Adding to the decor of Joel's room was a framed acrostic that said:

JOEL IS:

T all
H ungry
A dmirable
N ifty
K ind
S ki Champion
G ood Looking
I ntelligent
V ery Unique
I mpressive
N ice Personality
G ood Example

Friends have taken the acrostic idea and made it for their preteen and teen's birthday, using the first name for the acrostic:

HAPPY BIRTHDAY

D ynamic
E nergetic
B asketball Star
B eautiful
I ndustrious
E nthusiastic!

This special gift of praise conveys to our preteens (and all the friends that frequent their rooms): "Mom thinks I am full of positive qualities—maybe I am!"

Let me add a word of caution. As your adolescents get older, they may not be so excited about displaying your artwork on their wall. One day you may walk in and find some of them missing. Don't get upset; that's just the normal progression. They have served their purpose and have been a reminder that mom thinks they are special. Your message of encouragement will continue long after the room decor has changed!

The Red Plate

One Christmas we received a much-prized gift from our special friends, the Dillows. It was a beautiful red ceramic plate that says, "YOU ARE VERY SPECIAL TODAY." It has become one of our most treasured possessions.

When do we use The Red Plate? Birthdays, Mother's Day, Father's Day. When Jonathan wins in a tennis match, when Jonathan loses a tennis match, when Joel gets an A on a test, when Joel studied hard for a test but studied all the wrong things. You get the point. We use it for special days and for days that desperately need to be special.

You can find The Red Plate in most Christian bookstores or you can create your own. One friend loved the idea and discovered a red plate and cup at a pottery factory for $1.00. It was christened in their home the day their son had a bike accident and chipped both front teeth. Barely able to eat, his dinner was served on The Red Plate and his milk in The Red Cup. (You can order these plates directly by writing: The Original Red Plate Company, P.O. Box 7965, Newport Beach, CA 92660.)

Notes of Praise

Simple yet significant are the frequent notes left for our offsprings. In the kitchen I have a drawer in which I keep index cards, a felt tip pen and stickers. Some of the stickers give the messages "Fantastic!", "Grade A," "Out of Sight." With the investment of a minute or two, a note of praise can brighten any preteen's day! Sample notes are included. Use these or create your own. You'll be the winner as your child gets the message, "I am special. I am a person of worth. My mom believes in me!"

- "Congratulations! Knew you could ace that test!"
- "Jack, know you feel bad about the geography test. It's a real bummer to study hard and not do well. I admire your good study habits and think you are super. Better luck next time!"
- "Know it was disappointing to lose the soccer game, but with your good attitude, you're a winner anyway!"

Again, a reminder, be sensitive to the time when your kids begin to feel they are too old for mom's cute notes! For several years I would decorate Jonathan's lunch napkin with a note and a sticker. He loved them and carefully peeled each sticker off and decorated his lunch box. By the end of the school year all you could see was a collage of stickers. Message? Mom loves me and thinks I am neat!

Seventh grade came and no longer were stickers and notes in vogue; he no longer took a lunchbox but had graduated to the junior high brown bag. Dave was unaware of this change so once when I was out of town and he was fixing lunches, he included the old sticker-note routine. My, did he ever hear about it! So be sensitive. We want to encourage our kids, not embarrass them!

Letter of Praise

A birthday, a happy event, a sad event all can be good times to write a letter of praise. One friend wrote a birthday letter to her thirteen year old, expressing all the areas of growth she had seen since the twelfth birthday. Another mother wrote a letter as her son graduated from high school, expressing her faith in him and emphasizing two gifts she had tried to give to her son, the gift of roots and of wings.

I wrote the following letter to Jarrett on his sixteenth birthday:

Dear Jarrett,

On the occasion of your sixteenth birthday, we want to share with you sixteen things we admire about you.

1. Pleasing personality
2. Sensitivity to others
3. Commitment to our family
4. Inquisitive mind
5. Boldness in sharing your faith
6. Spiritual sensitivity to God
7. Wittiness and good sense of humor
8. Neatness and organization
9. Leadership ability
10. Willingness to stand alone in the midst of peer pressure
11. Academic excellence
12. Athletic ability
13. Good sportsmanship
14. Honesty and truthfulness
15. Commitment to God
16. Being a good model for others to follow

We want you to know we love and appreciate you. Happy Birthday!

Love,
Mom and Dad

Special Person Party

Parties are expected on birthdays and other important days but a "special person party" is given for no reason at all except to say "I love you; you are special." It can be simple or elaborate, with gifts or without. The structure is not important, the message is! Here is one mom's story:

The big track meet was in two weeks and Carl had practiced for months. It was to be the highlight of his sophomore year. Three days before the meet he landed incorrectly while high jumping and broke his arm. Did his world fall in? You bet it did!

The family rallied together. I made his favorite dinner, his sister baked and decorated a cake which said, "Carl, you are our Super Star." We made posters that said: "We admire your spirit!" "Next Year's Track Champ," and "We love Carl." We each gave him a coupon stating something that we would do for him.

Did this party erase the disappointment he felt? No. But it did express that we understood and felt his hurt and that we were on his team.

Easing the Hard Knocks

Our lives are sprinkled with disappointments, hurts, and frustrations. The adolescent years are times that are especially vulnerable to hurts and hard knocks. If we are willing to sprinkle our adolescents' lives generously with encouragement and concentrate on their good points, we can be positive reinforcing agents who say, "You are very special. You are a person of value. I'm so glad I'm your mom!"

Now it's your turn. Commit yourself to building up your preteen by completing exercise 3.

EXERCISE 3

Building Up Your Preteen

I. Keep a record of the positive and negative statements you say to your teen for the next twenty-four hours.

II. Give your teen one honest compliment each day this week. List things for which you could compliment your teen.

1. Compassion + Kindness

2. leadership qualities

3. nice personal grooming

4. loving attitude toward family

5. Honesty + truthfulness

6. Inquisitive mind

III. Plan and write down one praise project you are going to do this week, such as: write a letter, make an acrostic, have a special person's party.

7. Creativeness

8. Happy, pleasing personality

Chapter Five

GETTING OFF
THE LECTURE CIRCUIT

"I'm a good student, chairman of the debate team, and a starter on the basketball team," one teenage boy told me. "You'd think my mom would be proud of me. When I was nominated for student body president, I was really excited. I came right home and told mom. She said, 'That's nice, now change your clothes, so you can wash the car. You didn't do it yesterday.' She's always too busy to listen."

A teenage girl's experience was not much different. "I open up and talk to my mom. She thinks she listens, but she really just waits for an opening so she can give me morality lecture no. 395. I just have to stand there and wait for the benediction!"

If these teens are right, some moms don't spend much time listening to their teenagers. I've found that you can't have a good relationship with your teen or preteen if you don't listen to your child. My advice would be: Listen, don't lecture.

Think about your best friend. Would you be too busy to listen to her? Would you give her a sermon when you didn't agree? Would you correct her grammar when she told you a story?

We long for our children to communicate, but when they do, we're often too preoccupied with thoughts of our own. We see their mouths moving, we nod and say the appropriate "really," "uh huh," but our minds and hearts are miles away. One young boy who was competing with his siblings for mom's attention held her face in his hands so she had to look at him and listen to what he said. Our preteens won't go to this extreme but they need our full attention when they talk to us.

Sometimes just the opposite is true. We listen to our preteens and teens too intently, analyzing each thing they say. When we think we see any rebellious or abnormal tendencies, we panic. Since teens love the shock effect, we moms are often their guinea pigs.

A CASE IN POINT

I had pulled my shoulder in a tennis match and was in great pain as Jarrett began to tell me about a conversation with Mr. Brown, a teacher he not only liked but admired. Mr. Brown had said, "The Bible is written by men and has many contradictions. Sure it has a lot of good things in it, but you just can't accept all that it contains."

Now a sick feeling in the pit of my stomach, which came from feelings of parental failure, joined the pain radiating from my shoulder. At the ripe age of fourteen, was Jarrett ready to shuck all my husband and I had taught him because Mr. Brown believed differently?

Somehow I managed to listen without openly showing panic. I remember saying something like, "That's an interesting subject. Where did Mr. Brown get his information? We have several books that deal with this subject—perhaps you would like to study them. We could even choose one to go through as a family. It's important for each of us to know what we believe and why. I wouldn't want you to base your belief in Scripture on what I say or doubt the Bible based on what Mr. Brown has to say. You need to examine the facts for yourself!"

Then silently I sent a giant SOS to God and asked Him to help me trust Him and not blow it or attack Jarrett or Mr. Brown. How hard it is for me to trust when it seems all I have tried to instill in my teen is suddenly going down the drain!

Later I gave some books to Jarrett. His response to my

suggestion that he browse through them was, "Oh, Mom, I really do believe in the authority of the Scriptures. I just wanted to see how a Christian would react to someone who believed differently." I'd passed this test and felt great about it.

We did follow up this episode by going through Josh McDowell's excellent book, *Answers to Tough Questions*, (Here's Life Publishers) as a family. We discussed one question each morning at breakfast. This gave us all a better understanding of the "whys" behind some of our beliefs.

Listen, Don't React

Perhaps, you, too, have to work on actively listening to your preteen. We do need to listen but many times we overreact to what we hear. In James 1:19, we are told to: "listen much, speak little, and not become angry" (TLB). I've memorized this verse and repeat it in my mind when I'm tempted to respond too quickly.

It's a privilege to have a young person ask your opinion. However, a few poor responses may discourage any future sharing, so be careful. Some mothers have learned to answer a question with another question, which starts teens thinking on their own. Notice the desired reaction to one smart mother's technique. "My mom has this wonderful way of getting through. She doesn't say, 'You should' when I need help with a decision, but 'Have you considered...?' or 'Maybe this would work...' giving me the final choice. And she lets me rattle on with just enough encouragement, until I sort things out."[1]

No Advice, Please

Often when our teens talk to us, they don't necessarily want our opinions; they're only asking us to listen.

One teen said, "My mom says she is always willing to listen but she takes what I say and uses it as a launching pad for a lecture. I told her a friend was experimenting with drugs and I wanted to know how to help her. She started into a big lecture on 'teenage drugs, how awful' as if I was the one experimenting! Why does a friendly talk always have to turn into an object lesson? I just wanted to help my friend."

When our children talk to us, they want us to hear them out completely with no interruptions. Once we begin to listen with open minds and closed mouths, we can listen for feelings.

I'll never forget my distress when Joel told our youngest son, Jonathan, "Go to bed. I want to talk to our parents." At that point I didn't know what was ahead, but I braced myself for whatever was coming, obviously something that couldn't be shared with a younger brother.

"You know, spring break's coming soon," Joel began. "Some of the guys and I want to go to Florida together."

Joel was sixteen at the time, and Dave and I weren't prepared for this pitch for independence quite so soon.

"Maybe all of us could go together," I suggested after a long pause in which I had thought of several responses and rejected all the others. "You know, the whole family. Maybe Jarrett might even be home from college then."

Joel shifted his weight from one foot to the other, cleared his throat, and said, "Mom, it's not our house I want to get away from. It's the contents."

That statement threw me for a moment. I started to say, "Well, that's a great thing to say," then I stopped. What feelings were we hearing? First, it was obvious Joel wanted a break from his family. Did he really dislike us, or was it just a cry for independence?

"Give Mom and me a chance to think about it," Dave replied, which gave us all an opportunity to cool down.

That night as Dave and I discussed the idea, we thought of a possible solution. Paul, the twenty-three-year-old Campus Crusade for Christ team member who led Joel's action group and Bible study, just might go with the boys.

"They'd accept him," Dave said. "They all enjoy being with him, and we can trust his supervision."

Did this negotiation take a lot of time? You bet it did. Along the way, Joel looked upward and jokingly said, "They're great parents, God, but sometimes I wish I had the kind who doesn't care."

Paul and six teenage boys spent five days at Gulf Shores in Alabama. They had a great time and, although Joel has never admitted it, Paul was a major contributor to their fun. They spent long hours on the beach; they rented a VCR and overdosed on fifteen movies. Later Paul commented, "I don't think I had the control you think I had." Still Joel had enjoyed as much freedom as we felt he could handle.

I've found that the key to dealing with this kind of situation is being able to listen for the feelings underneath a child's statement.

Listen for Feelings

Listening for feelings means that Mom doesn't evaluate, offer advice, analyze, or ask tons of questions, admittedly hard to pull off. She listens with her mouth clamped shut, then feeds back a comment that lets her teen know she is trying to understand what he means and how he feels.

Teen: "Melanie is a complete nerd, she's two-faced and a fake."

Mom (Normal response): "How do you know Melanie is a fake and two-faced? How would you like to be called a nerd? God tells us not to judge and to love others unconditionally."

If Mom is listening for feelings, she might respond like this, however:

Mom: "Sounds like you and Melanie are on the outs. It really hurts when friends seem to turn against you."

Stop for a moment and think. Isn't it wonderful when

someone really understands and cares how you feel? We can handle pressure better if we know even one other person understands. We can be that "other person" for our children if we are willing to listen—not lecture, react, or advise—and identify with their feelings. Save your advice for the family dog!

PHYSICAL SPACE NEEDED

Not only do we meet many moms of preteens who are "natural lecturers," but also many who have a natural talent for other people's business, specifically in their own families. As one man said, "Women's curiosity and imagination are monumental, and the way they can make an award-winning adventure out of an everyday happening leaves us men gasping in astonishment."

Every strength has its weakness, and we moms must restrain our craving for knowledge about our teenagers. If we are communicating, we don't have to read our daughter's diary, letters, and notes or look in our son's private drawer or locked box to check on behavior. We might get information but it's not worth the lack of trust.

A Reformed Snooper

"I was addicted to snooping," one woman admitted to me. "I investigated every dirty jeans pocket, every crushed piece of paper. I have even been known to spend up to an hour scotch-taping a mutilated note back together. Am I a Christian? Oh, yes! Was I wrong? Oh, yes! Am I reformed? Hopefully!"

Perhaps our young peoples' rooms, desks, diaries, and dirty jeans pockets should be labeled: "Snooping not allowed! Snoopers will be prosecuted!" Our teens need privacy; they need to be given space.

How can we handle our curiosity? When our boys began to enter the adolescent world, Dave and I began to pray that God would show us the important mistakes they were making. Our prayers have been answered. It's amazing the little tips He has given us: a cigarette left on the couch; a comment from another mom, "Oh, yes, your son is known as the 'Dirty word dictionary.'" God has been so faithful in this area that we don't want to know what we don't need to know. Now as our teens are approaching the adult years, from time to time they share with us some of the things they did when they were thirteen and fourteen. We are thankful for guardian angels, and we are also thankful we did not know everything!

A word to the wise might be added at this point. The early adolescent years (ages twelve-fourteen) often bring with them a fascination for dirty words and gross sex terms. If you accidentally find a filthy note, don't panic! You have not failed at motherhood. Do not take this note as evidence that your kid is into sex or drugs. If you found it legitimately (like the time I found one on the kitchen floor!), you can use it to open a discussion as to appropriate language and God's view of sex and thought control. But remember to "listen much, speak little, and not become angry" (TLB).

When Joel was thirteen, we heard some unofficial reports that he was using bad language at school. I mentioned my concern in a letter to a trusted friend who had older teens. Her response was very helpful. She wrote:

> My feeling is there's a 99 percent chance it's very temporary, and he'll do it a few times to get attention. We don't expect our kids never to make a mistake. But there's always a sick, scary feeling when we learn that our kid has misbehaved; we are afraid every mistake will turn into a lifetime habit....Instead of confronting him personally, why not discuss the use of bad language in your family devotions?

We tried this, but Dave eventually had to confront Joel directly. He replied, "Dad, what if I promise not to use any more bad language as your birthday present?"

Dave heartily agreed. And Joel kept his word. This promise was one of the best presents Dave ever received.

Your Own Corner

During the preadolescent years, the three Arp brothers shared a large room. It was partitioned into three cubicles but was still one big room. When Jarrett turned thirteen, we saw his need for space and privacy from two younger brothers.

Our solution was to give Jarrett a new room on his fourteenth birthday, moving Dave's office to the den to provide the space for Jarrett. This privacy greatly improved the relationship between the Arp brothers, but wasn't this inconvenient for Dave? Yes, we all had to flex, but it was worth it.

It's not always possible to find or build rooms in our homes. However, we have decided that wherever we live with our teens, we will somehow create their own corner. Teens need a place to call their own, even if that means building walls and making one bedroom into two or using room dividers or bookcases. Privacy and space contribute to good communication.

EMOTIONAL SPACE NEEDED

Our teens also need emotional space because they are noted for their mood changes. Psychologists tell us it takes a lot of energy to control their impulses as they strive for independence. They are more behavior-oriented than verbal, since they haven't yet mastered good communication skills. At times they are argumentative and irritable.

Are you willing, Mom, to back up and resist the urge to correct every angry countenance? Are you willing to let your adolescent vent emotions? Home is one place where kids should be able to blow it and still be loved and accepted. As one of our teens commented, "Home is where you prepare for the battle, not where you fight the battle."

One mother told the women in her Moms' Support Group, "I'll never forget the day Bob came in the door, threw his books on the kitchen table, and exploded, 'My dumb math teacher gave us a surprise test today, and I know I flunked! I hate him. I hate school. I am going to just give up!' "

What was this mom's reaction? If she were giving her teen emotional space, she would say, "Sounds like your day was a real bummer." Unfortunately, this mom, like many of us, flunked this test the first time. After the discussion that day, however, she decided that every slammed door and every angry word doesn't need to be corrected.

Allow the luxury of venting some emotions. Why not practice First Corinthians 13:5: "Love does not hold grudges and will hardly even notice when others do it wrong" (TLB).

Remember what I said in the first chapter: "Moms must change in order to remain the same loving parent." Here is a good example. Now we focus on our teens as friends and less as our children. Since we are beginning to let them assume some responsibility for their actions, we are not obligated to correct every fault we see.

There is a balance here. I am not saying that our pre-teens should habitually be able to slam doors or hurl angry words our way. Neither should they be allowed to be really disrespectful. However, often parents ride too hard on their kids because they're afraid they'll lose control. As a result, the teen is not given the real opportunity to express feelings.

Recently Jonathan was visiting a home where there are several teenagers. His comment when I came to get him made me glad we have chosen to give our boys some emotional space.

"You wouldn't believe it, Mom," he said. "Jim's parents

never listen to how he feels about anything. They just state their case and say, 'That's the way it is. No discussion.' I sure would hate to live in their home."

Dave and I have found that allowing the teen emotional space is the first step in making the transition from the vertical parent/child relationship to the horizontal friendship, which exists between parents and adult children. Remember, friendship is based on two individuals relating to each other as peers, not as one being superior and the other inferior.

A friend of mine sadly related how her own relationship with her mother never changed from the parent-child relationship to a friend-to-friend relationship, even though she is now thirty-eight and has two children of her own.

"To mom, I'm still her little girl," she told me. "She gets upset if I try to build an open relationship and share opinions and feelings with her that are different from her own. To disagree, in her eyes, is to be disrespectful. After all, she is my mother. How I wish she could also be my friend!"

It's too bad this mother didn't learn to allow her daughter to voice some of her opinions in her teen years. How different their relationship might be today.

Drawing Out Your Preteen

What about the adolescent who clams up and just won't talk? The adolescent years have been described as a period when youngsters don't talk to the family, live in the clutter they call a room, and come out three times a day to eat and grunt at the family. What can we do to foster communication?

Merton and Irene Strommen asked the 8,165 young adolescents in their study, "For each of the following five items, tell if it is something you want to talk about with your parents more, less, or the same as you do now." Participants in the survey were then to answer this question for issues relating to drugs, friends, school, ideas of right and wrong, and sex.[2]

They found that "Young adolescents...are more parent-oriented than peer-oriented. They prefer being able to talk with their parents about issues that bother them. Grade five is a time of special opportunity for parents to help the young adolescent initiate conversations and learn how to communicate on a feeling level."[3]

However, the Strommens noted, "Youth's interest in discussing adolescent issues with their parents steadily declines between fifth grade (58 percent) and ninth grade (37 percent). The number who want more communication with their parents on five youth topics shows a marked decline."[4]

Take advantage of the precious preteen years. Then adopt these three communication techniques for those teen years when a child is less likely to share his or her ideas with you.

Watch for open gates. Teens often want to talk to us at the most inconvenient time—when the toast is about to burn, when we're tired and want a couple of minutes alone to regroup, late at night, right before guests are to arrive.

One of our sons got home from his very first prom at 2 A.M. The evening had been super! As he sat on the side of our bed he spilled out all the exciting details, on and on until all I wanted to do was sleep! Finally I said, "Tell me the rest in the morning!" You guessed it, the day-after conversation never happened. Two A.M. was the open gate, not the morning after.

When our children were younger it was easy to plan communication times, all we had to do was ask them to go out for ice cream. Not so with teens! Some of their friends might just see them, and to be caught out with Mom would be social suicide for a fourteen year old. I remember asking Joel at age fifteen to go out for a banana split; he has been an ice cream freak for years, but he said no. So what's a mom to do?

Start looking for open gates, and once the gate begins to open, help keep it open by comments like: "Really?" "You did, huh?" "Interesting!" "Tell me more about it." "I'd be interested in your point of view." Statements like these give our teens a chance to really open up to us. Many times our teen turtles poke out their necks to test and see if it is safe to say what they really feel. This may be done by making a shocking statement; and if mother does not react, they can continue. If a lecture results, they retreat back into their shell.

Find communication centers. Several years ago the Arp family moved into a new house. Perhaps you've experienced that lost feeling of not knowing where anything is or where to put things you are unpacking. Settling in is much more than arranging furniture and the kitchen. It's also discovering those special places that foster communication.

In our present home it's our den; if I'm sitting there, our teens will usually come and join me. Conversations just seem to open up easier in front of the fireplace than in the kitchen where I'm usually doing five things at once. There is also no television in our den.

To test my theory I did an experiment once. I casually said to Joel, who had been in his shell all week, "I appreciate your always being honest with me and open in our relationship." This was the bait. Then I went to the den. Soon Joel appeared on the scene, and two hours later we were still talking, having been joined by his older brother.

Perhaps in your home it's your bedroom or your teen's room. Stop for a minute and think about where communication flows easily. Then plan to be there frequently with a listening ear.

Find communication activities. Sports have played an important role in building communication in our family. You would probably laugh if you saw me skiing down the slopes with our boys. I learned to ski when I was in my thirties, a time when any self-respecting mom would be sitting in the coffee shop.

But as I'm shivering on a chairlift ride with the boys or trying to get down a scary slope, our relationships soar. The cold feet and sore muscles are worth it. So are the sore muscles from a game of tennis doubles with the three Arp teens. We slug it out on the court and then sit together afterwards, sweaty and tired, and laugh over everything that happened. To be honest, there have also been disasters with bad calls and angry losers, but the good times are more frequent than the bad.

I'm not saying that you have to become a "jock" when your children become preteens, but in our family, sports have provided a backdrop for communication and deeper sharing. So, I imagine, would shopping with girls, singing with musical teens, studying computer programs with computer wizards.

Have you made your preteen's interests yours? It takes work; skiing did not come easily for me. I was not athletic before I gave birth to three boys, but sports have opened the communication gates in our home. What will open yours?

Stop now and complete exercise 4, which will turn the theory of this chapter into action at your home.

EXERCISE 4

Getting Off The Lecture Circuit

 I. How can you give your preteen or teen space in your relationship?

   A. Physically?

   B. Emotionally?

 II. Where does most communication take place in your home?

III. What activities do you have in common with your preteen or teen, which will foster communication?

IV. What activities would you like to develop?

 V. Determine this week to listen without reacting, lecturing, or giving advice.

VI. Memorize James 1:19.
"It is best to listen much, speak little, and not become angry."

Chapter Six

WHEN THE BRIDGE IS OUT

Muffled voices drifted into my subconscious and woke me up. "Hi, what ya doing?" "You'll never believe it." "It's really cool." "Want to...?"

I rolled over in bed and rubbed my eyes. The time? I looked at the luminescent dial on our clock radio; it read 12:30 A.M. Was I dreaming? It might have been a nightmare but not a dream; the voices that I still heard were outside the window next to ours, Jarrett's window.

Irritation began to escalate as I thought, *It's not fair. I work long hours as a mother of teens each day and at night I deserve my sleep!* I stormed out of bed and into Jarrett's room.

Immediately I launched into a lecture on inconsideration, how I needed my sleep, and the inappropriateness of late night visitors and late night noise. Then I noticed a rope close by the window.

"What are you going to use that rope for anyway? Rappelling out the window, by chance?" I launched into my favorite lecture on trust. Angry words having been unloaded, I retreated back to bed.

The next morning I wondered how I could rebuild the bridge I'd burned in the early morning hours. What had I done wrong? I'd hurled accusations and let my anger get out of control. The list could go on and on.

I had also ignored the good advice I had just read in *Between Parent and Teenager*. Dr. Ginott gives these three principles:

1. Don't attack personality attributes.
2. Don't criticize character traits.
3. Deal with the situation at hand.

Dr. Ginott continues with this advice, "When things go wrong, it is not the right time to tell a teenager anything about his personality or character. When a person is drowning, it is not a good time to teach him to swim or to ask him questions or criticize his performance. It is a time to help!"[1]

We can apply all we've learned about listening, identifying feelings, and promoting conversations, but the communication bridge will still frequently sag and occasionally burn down. It is hard to face failures, especially when we're trying. We're all human, so what can we do when we or our children blow it? In the following pages I will give you some tips on how to combat several kinds of bridge failures.

WHEN MOM CAUSES THE COMMUNICATION FAILURE

Nothing could change the fact that I had blown it, but what could I do to rebuild the bridge I'd burned down the night before? The first thing I needed to do was to apologize. To Jarrett I said, "I was wrong to hurl accusations, to vent my anger at you, and not to listen. It wasn't your fault that your friends came by at 12:30 A.M. Will you forgive me?"

Secondly, I decided to offer a helping hand as he was refinishing a piece of furniture to earn extra money. Stripping paint rates in my popularity book about where I put stripping unstrippable wallpaper. It was hard work, but as we were sanding we were also stripping our negative feelings, which had been the bridge burners the night before. Also, by my positive actions, I was showing my son that I was on his team.

If I had actually caught Jarrett using that rope to rappel down the side of our house, obviously I would have taken a different course of action. Sneaking out of the house in the middle of the night is a major offense in our house and in that of most families. We'll talk about dealing with major issues in chapter 8.

We don't have to live with burned bridges. They can be

repaired, but it's usually up to us to take the first step.

Learning to Say, 'I'm Sorry'

I am still learning how important it is to apologize in the right way. My natural tendency is to point the finger and make excuses for myself, to say, "Jarrett, I couldn't help being angry last night because I was tired and besides you weren't very understanding. But, will you forgive me?" Using the apology as an opportunity to lecture is a mistake.

Instead, we need to name our fault: "I hurled insults and vented my anger on you. Will you forgive me?" We should not remind our teen what he or she did wrong or ask, "Now, don't you have something to say to me?"

The failure is between the teen and God. If the parent is a good example, then the young person will eventually learn to do the same. Often when I've eaten humble pie, my teens have also asked for forgiveness. If mom can, they can too!

WHEN TEENS CAUSE COMMUNICATION FAILURE

Preteens and teens often close the communication lines when they are frustrated or angry after dealing with a situation they do not know how to handle. Picture the following scene:

Mom: "What's wrong, Meagan?"

Meagan: "He's a creep, a first class dork! Why did I ever want to go with him?!"

Mom: "You sound angry, what happened?"

Meagan: "I don't want to talk about it, just leave me alone."

Meagan storms into her room, slams the door, turns the music up ten decibels, and stays in her room for hours. Meagan is obviously hurt, but Mom is hurt, too, at being closed out of her daughter's life.

When the adolescent causes the failure, often the verbal abuse ricochets and hits mom who is not really the cause of the anger but who just happens to be there to get the brunt of the situation. How can she possibly rebuild this bridge when she wasn't the one who burned it in the first place? A starting place is learning to forgive, even when not asked to.

Be a Forgiver

We moms need to be willing to forgive preteens and teens for hurting us with their caustic words, even when they don't seek forgiveness from us. Christ is our example as He forgave those who were crucifying Him. Remember, no relationship can continue without forgiveness, and moms are the adults in this situation.

One friend who has a very rocky history with her daughter says, "I start each day with a fresh slate. I wipe away all the previous day's hurts and angry verbal attacks each morning and give my daughter the opportunity to start over again."

Doesn't it hurt my friend when her daughter is unkind to her? Of course it does, but she has not allowed her hurts to damage the relationship. Once we get to the place where we can deal with our own hurts and forgive our teen, we can look at the situation more objectively. Sometimes a note will open up the communication.

Meagan's mom handled the situation by writing the following note, which was on Meagan's desk the next day.

Dear Meagan,

You really looked nice this morning in your new blouse. You have a real knack for putting clothes together. I know it hurts to have someone disappoint you. I have been praying about the situation with Rob and know you'll use wisdom in handling it. I'm so thankful God gave you to me as my daughter!

I love you,
Mom

P.S. My ear is open if you want to talk!

Meagan's mom communicated her trust, her love, and her desire to help, but she didn't push herself on Meagan. Her postscript let her teen know she was available.

Perhaps you're wondering how preteens and teens respond to such notes and letters. Some may give you a hug and tell you they love you. Others may not mention your "epistle of love," but don't be surprised if they put it away for safekeeping. I don't write letters to get a response; I write, forgive without being asked, rub backs, and drive car-pools because I love my teens and want to be the mother God desires me to be.

Breathing Room, Please!

There are times when our young people simply need some breathing room and not a hovering spirit named "Mom." If I wrote a note with every upset, my boys would soon tune me out.

Perhaps you are like me and prefer to have everything neatly packaged and in order, but that's just not always possible or healthy. When adolescents wrestle with hard situations and broken relationships, we desperately want to jump in and help; but sometimes the best way is to give our children emotional space.

No one that I know of has come up with the perfect formula for relating to any other human being, much less a changing adolescent. Only God can give us wisdom to discern when to write a note and when to give space. In James 1:5, we are told, "If any of you lack wisdom, let him ask of God, who gives to all liberally and without reproach, and it will be given."

That verse is very comforting to me as I seek to relate to my teens. It is also good to know that God never gets weary of my asking Him for wisdom. He doesn't say, "Oh, here comes Claudia again. Didn't I give her wisdom last week!" His wisdom is continually available for me and for you.

WHEN "NO!" THREATENS TO STOP A COMMUNICATION

All parents are asked to give permission to their children when the only answer must be, "No!" A typical instance from the Arp family archives began after a fantastic weekend. Joel and Jarrett had been at a church high school retreat, Jonathan had stayed with friends, and Dave and I had had a wonderful time at a friend's vacation home in the mountains. During part of this time we had evaluated our family situation and set future family goals. We had felt good about our teens, and the time had been affirming.

Table talk at dinner that Sunday evening was soaring when Joel dropped the bomb. One new skill he had learned from friends at the retreat was how to chew and dip tobacco. We didn't mind, did we?

Having just moved to the States from Austria, we weren't familiar with the local "cool" pastimes, so this one was a real shocker. How could Joel put that terrible stuff in his mouth? What would my friends think? After all, I was aspiring to write a book on preparing for the teen years.

"Joel, did you really enjoy it?" I questioned incredulously.

"It was great, except the dipping made my lip a little sore."

"What do you mean, dipping?" I asked. I'd never known anyone who chewed tobacco.

"You put a little bit of snuff between your lip and your gum, like this, Mom." Joel pulled his lip down to show me.

Surely this conversation is not happening to us, I thought as Jarrett added his comments, "Detestable! Repulsive!" *Have I succeeded with one and failed with the other?* I thought. "I don't see what's so bad about chewing. Everyone's doing it," Joel replied to Jarrett's comments, wisely dropping the campaign to dip and concentrating on winning "chewing rights." To strengthen his case, he spit out an impressive list of his Christian friends and elders in local churches who also chewed.

I was ready categorically to assume the role of judge and jury in this case, when Dave stepped in, encouraging Joel to tell us exactly how he felt.

"It really was a lot of fun, and it's not dangerous like smoking," Joel explained. "It's just not a moral issue in East Tennessee. I don't see any problem with it."

We continued the discussion a little longer, and then Dave said, "Joel, we realize this is something you really want to do, but as you can tell, we really have a problem with it. Let's drop it for now, but please refrain from chewing until we know more about it."

Joel agreed to this temporary injunction. "Well, I won't chew if you say I can't, but I still don't see anything wrong with it."

It would be pure fiction to say the issue ended here; for months, chewing was a hot topic at the Arps. I researched smokeless tobacco and produced the results of a 1979 study by Arden G. Christen, chairman of the preventive dentistry department at Indiana University.

"Dr. Arden found that nine of fourteen college athletes who chewed tobacco regularly had white patches in their mouths, where the tobacco touches the gum. Doctors believe this is a condition which probably causes cancer."

Joel still wasn't convinced, and I couldn't find much else to substantiate parental suspicions about the harmful effects of chewing.

It's much easier to say, "No, you can't do that. Issue ended!" The issue may be ended, but so is the communication. Throughout this whole ordeal, we let Joel express his feelings. At the same time, he valued our relationship enough not to chew, at least most of the time.

The next summer Joel's soccer team played in a tournament in England and Joel was able to visit his friends in Vienna, Austria, before the tournament. This was a great opportunity for Joel to be salt and light to his "pagan buddies," as he had really grown in his walk with the Lord since moving back to the States. Therefore it was a real shocker when a transatlantic phone call from his hostess began, "Claudia, there's a problem with Joel. It seems he brought along chewing tobacco and has been sharing with his friends. The parents here are in an uproar. One mom said, 'Isn't it sad that Joel has gone downhill spiritually after moving back to America?' "

Waiting for Dave to come home that hot July day, I vented my hurt, anger, and frustration on every weed in my vegetable garden. By the time Dave got home, I could at least discuss "his" son and the chewing fiasco without an ocean of tears.

It cost over one hundred dollars in phone bills to straighten out the situation with Joel, but we had to clear up some misunderstandings and convince him once again to be a nonchewer.

Did that settle the issue? Perhaps, who knows for sure? After returning from Vienna, Joel began to spend less time with his chewing buddies and to develop some new relationships. He became active in a Bible study and spent the next summer on a mission project in the Bahamas.

Would he still like to chew? Maybe. Joel will still argue that chewing is relatively safe. But not his brother Jonathan. I can thank a courageous mother in Oklahoma for that.

In 1984, Betty Ann Marsee sued a tobacco company for selling the "defective and unreasonably dangerous" product snuff, which her son used from the time he was twelve until his death from cancer of the mouth at age nineteen. Cancer destroyed the boy's tongue, his throat, and his jaw. Dr. Carl Hook, the boy's doctor, attributes the cancer to Sean's use of snuff.

Mrs. Marsee's suit sparked many articles in magazines like *Time, Business Week,* and *The Saturday Evening Post,* which brought out some of the ill effects for which Dave and

I had been searching. Here are some of these facts, which I shared with Jonathan and which might help you convince your child to steer clear of smokeless tobacco.

Your preteen or teen, like most kids, probably believes that smokeless tobacco really isn't harmful and is a safe alternative to smoking. Yet researcher Elbert Glover of East Carolina University in Greenville, North Carolina, says that "The nicotine level in the blood is higher in smokeless tobacco users than smokers." He has found that some would-be quitters were so addicted they "couldn't even stop for half a day."[2]

Some young people will admit, "You might have a problem if you dipped or chewed for many years," but they argue that short-term use is O.K. However, Arden Christen, the dentist whose earlier study I had mentioned to Joel, says, "Dipping causes visible damage in as little as three to four months. The gums may recede, the teeth loosen, biting surfaces are abraded....After several years the mouth can be devastated."[3]

If your teenager still has doubts, I recommend that you photocopy the pictures that appeared in the article, "Getting Tough on Snuff," in the September 1985 issue of the *Saturday Evening Post*. Several before-and-after photographs of young Sean Marsee show the tragic effects of smokeless tobacco on this young track star, who was named the outstanding athlete of his high school in 1983 and died one year later. Another photograph shows the grotesque mouth of an Indian woman who chewed tobacco regularly for ten years.

Scare tactics? Maybe. But Gregory Connolly, director of the dental division of the Massachusetts Department of Public Health, declares, "There is a chemical time bomb ticking in the mouths of hundreds of thousands of boys in this country."[4]

His antisnuff crusade led to a law requiring that *every* package of moist snuff sold in Massachusetts be labeled,

"Warning: Use of snuff can be addictive and can cause mouth cancer and other mouth disorders."

Dave and I know we were right to say no to Joel when he began chewing. We have learned, however, that how we handle a situation determines whether or not communication is broken.

WHEN YOU HAVE TO SAY "NO!"

Here are seven ways to keep communication open when you have to say "No!" to your teen:

1. It's really important to listen and be willing to identify with the teen's feelings. Let the adolescent say how he or she feels as long as it is done in an appropriate way.

2. Be patient! How much easier it would have been to say "No, and that's final!" This approach could have resulted in loss of communication and secret chewing behind parents' backs. (Joel read this illustration and agreed!)

3. Keep things light. Let humor be a guest in every discussion. At one point we gave Joel a cartoon that pictured two boys wearing baseball gloves, sitting on a doorstep. One said, "I can never be a professional baseball player."

The other boy asked, "Why?"

The response: "I'm not allowed to spit!"

4. Continue to concentrate on the relationship. Don't allow the issue to become a "gloom cloud" over everything else.

5. If you become angry, proclaim a "cooling down period." When an issue comes up, if it's not urgent, wait twenty-four hours before dealing with it.

6. Don't allow yourself to get pulled into an issue right before a meal when your blood sugar and patience are both low.

7. Remember, a particular situation is probably temporary. If the issue is nonlife-threatening (dress codes, makeup,

hair styles), how important will it be in ten years? Then ask yourself, how much more important will the relationship be in ten years? *Deal with the issue as best you can, but do all you can to preserve the relationship.*

PREVENTING COMMUNICATION FAILURE

Both mom and teen need to work at preventing future bridge washouts. We have used the following principles in our family:

Avoid "You" statements. Statements that begin with the word *you* tend to attack others while *I* statements reflect back on the speaker and are much safer to use. Compare the difference between these statements:

"You make me so angry!" vs. "I am so angry!"
"You don't love me!" vs. "I really feel unloved!"

Avoid "Why" questions. Questions that begin with the word *why* often lead to broken bridges. For instance, "Why can't you be more considerate of me and pick up your mess in the TV room?" does not instill an attitude of cooperation. Better: "The TV room is something else. Do you think we could get it back in order?" The key is to attack the problem, not the personality.

Do express feelings. We talked earlier about the importance of listening for and identifying feelings as our teens are talking to us. Equally important is to express our feelings and help our kids express their own feelings. Here is a simple formula that we have utilized in our home, which also works well with your mate. Simply state how you feel about a given situation.

An example is, "I feel frustrated when food and dirty dishes are left in the TV room. It is extra work for me and would be so simple if each of us would pick up after himself."

Then say, "Tell me how you feel about this." This way

we can deal with the issue at hand, and our teen is not defensive. Often the response will be, "Gee, Mom, I'm sorry I left the mess. I'll try to remember next time." The issue has been confronted (messed-up TV room) and the relationship preserved.

When you must disagree with your teen, you could say something like this, "This may be the way you see it, but this is how I see it." Again you are expressing your feelings without attacking the person.

WHEN ANGER BLOCKS COMMUNICATION

Dr. David Mace states that the greatest cause of marital failure is not communication, but dealing with anger. Could this also be true in parent-teen relationships? We know all the communication skills, we are determined to use them, and then something happens to make us angry and all of our common sense goes out the window. If you've never been angry at your child this section is not for you, and I would like to meet you. Anger is a fact of life at our house. The question is: "How can we deal with anger in a constructive way without destroying the communication bridge?"

Learn to Be Angry

In Ephesians 4:26, we are told, "Be angry and do not sin." For many of us this may appear to be a contradiction, but if we're honest we'll admit that anger is a familiar visitor. Harsh words strain the bridge supports, and before we know it we're on opposite sides of the crevice with no way to cross over. Since anger is often around, how can we deal with anger without sinning?

Solomon put it this way, "A wise man controls his temper. He knows that anger causes mistakes." What is the balance? How can we handle our anger and train our teens to handle theirs in an appropriate way?

The Anger Ladder

In his book *How to Really Love Your Teenager*, Dr. Ross Campbell deals with different ways of handling anger in order of appropriateness. Since handling anger is a learned response, the more mature a person is the more maturely he will express his anger. However, some adults have never learned how to handle anger and are poor role models for their teens, yet they often expect adolescents to handle anger in an appropriate way or even not to express anger at all.[5]

Consider the following six levels of handling anger (see illustration 3). Number one is the worst way to handle anger and number six the most appropriate way. Picture a ladder with six rungs. The goal is to move up the ladder to a higher rung, so we learn better ways of dealing with our angry feelings. This is for both mom and teen!

Let's see how this anger ladder helps us better understand a real situation. It had been a fun doubles tennis match. Jonathan and I barely beat Jarrett and Joel and the conflict developed over the last play of the match. Jarrett had missed the point and Jonathan commented that he could have probably made the point. Jarrett, not appreciating this remark from his younger brother, began to give Jonathan some unsolicited advice. What a setup for testing the anger ladder! Jonathan will be our example here, but before telling you how he handled his anger, let's go through the six levels and see how he could have reacted.

Level 1—Passive aggressive behavior
This is the worst way to handle anger. Jonathan could have hidden his anger toward Jarrett, then later smashed Jarrett's new stereo.

Level 2—Out of control behaviorally
Jonathan could have gone into a fit of rage and actually destroyed property or become violent toward others, not

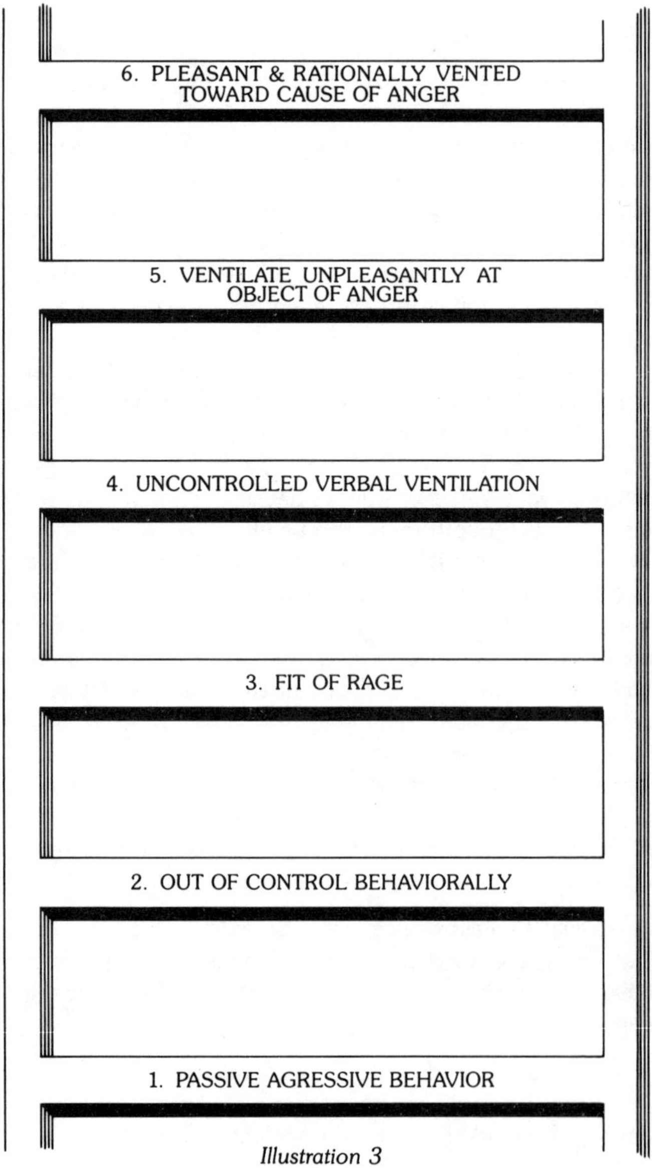

6. PLEASANT & RATIONALLY VENTED
TOWARD CAUSE OF ANGER

5. VENTILATE UNPLEASANTLY AT
OBJECT OF ANGER

4. UNCONTROLLED VERBAL VENTILATION

3. FIT OF RAGE

2. OUT OF CONTROL BEHAVIORALLY

1. PASSIVE AGRESSIVE BEHAVIOR

Illustration 3

necessarily the person he is angry at. In this case, Jonathan might have thrown his tennis racket down, stomped on it until it was broken, and slugged Jarrett, and even me, his innocent partner!

Level 3—Fit of rage

Jonathan could have yelled, screamed, and cursed at Jarrett in an attempt to hurt him verbally. He might have even started a verbal assault on Joel and me too.

Level 4—Uncontrolled verbal ventilation

Here Jonathan would still be out of control verbally but would not be attempting to hurt anyone. He would yell and scream and be generally very unpleasant. But note the progression. This is a much better way to handle anger than the previous three. He is not destroying property or being vindictive.

Level 5—Ventilate unpleasantly at object of anger

At this level, Jonathan would deal with his anger by perhaps yelling or crying but would confine his remarks to Jarrett and to the issue at hand: "I do not want advice on the tennis court."

Level 6—Pleasantly and rationally vented toward cause of anger

This, of course, would be the best way to handle his anger. At the time he could express his anger, "I am angry. I don't like it when you give me advice." Then later he and Jarrett could rationally discuss the issue and make some decision such as: "Next time we play tennis, let's confine our remarks to times we can honestly compliment each other. When we're practicing drills together, you can give me tips and advice."

Now I would like to tell you that Jonathan immediately handled his anger at level six, but actually he was more at level five. Rather than getting upset because he didn't handle his anger in the best way possible, I was pleased that he did so well.

Dr. Campbell states, "Resolving the issue means for both parties to rationally and logically examine the issue, discuss it, understand it from both points of view, and to come to an agreement on what to do about it. This takes a great deal of maturity on both sides. Few people ever come to this point of maturity in their lives."[6]

He goes on to challenge parents to be good examples in the expression of their own anger and to expect anger to be frequent when teens are present. "Instead of forbidding our teens from becoming angry or overreacting to their anger, we need to meet them where they are in handling their anger and train them from there." Our goal for ourselves and our teens is verbal expression of anger.[7]

HOW TO CLIMB THE LADDER

Several days after the tennis saga, the boys and I sat down and talked through the anger ladder and examined where on the ladder each of us was in this instance. We then talked about how we might have handled it at a higher level and decided to try this method next time we got into a head-to-head situation on the tennis courts.

In a calm time, either before anger attacks or after it subsides, go over the anger ladder either as a family or alone with your teen (see exercise 5). Discuss what is an appropriate reaction and how you handle anger now. Next time anger comes to your house, evaluate your response. Maybe your teen will say, "I'm at level four. Maybe next time I can move up a rung."

The best time to help our teen is when he is mad and angry at someone else, not at mom. Consider this conversation:

Bob: "I'm so angry at Jill. She promised to go to the

prom with me and now she said no. She's going with that airhead, Pete!"

Mom: "I see you are really irritated. If that happened to me, I'd feel hurt and let down."

When our teens are angry and upset, we need to let them talk without giving a lecture on how it is wrong to hate. They need someone to listen, but we don't have to solve everything for them. After their strong feelings evaporate, we can help them evaluate how they are handling their anger.

Am I saying, it's O.K. for our teens to hate? No. We have taught our guys since their toddler years to give a blessing for an insult. They know what the Scriptures say but there are times when we need to jog their memory gently. But if we try to monitor every fit of anger and correct every spoken word, sooner or later, we'll find our teens have tuned us out.

TO SUM IT UP

Burned bridges, whether burned by mom, by teen, by parents' having to say no, or by a fit of rage, don't have to remain a disaster. Reconstruction can start today, and it can start with you, Mom. You can begin by forgiving and then asking for forgiveness. You can jump over that crevice and get on the same side through a common communication activity or by writing a note or giving space. You can patiently listen for feelings and resist the role of judge. Any issue, light or heavy, is not really as important as the relationship. Again, ask yourself, "Will this problem be important in ten years? Will my relationship with my son or daughter be important then?" The obvious answer will help you regain your perspective.

EXERCISE 5

Rebuilding the Communication Bridge

  I. Think of a time that you have blown it. How could you have responded differently?

  II. This week practice using the feelings formula:
"Let me tell you how I feel....
(I feel frustrated, angry, happy, sad...)
"Now tell me how you feel."

 III. Go over the anger ladder with your preteen or as a family.
  A. Discuss appropriate ways of handling anger.

  B. Let each person identify where he or she generally is on the anger ladder.

 IV. Agree to work together to move up a rung on the ladder.

Chapter Seven

GOOD HOUSEKEEPING OR GROADY TO THE MAX

"It's all gray. Everything is gray!" Janice sobbed. "When the kids were younger, right was right, wrong was wrong. Black was black and white, white. Once they became teen-agers, the whole world looked gray, and all I did was make decisions—so many of them seemed to fall in that gray area. How important was the condition of my teen's clothes, hair, and room? Was it really wrong to be groady to the max? The Bible doesn't say, 'Thou shalt not wear jeans nor leave your clothes on the floor nor go to this party.' "

Can you relate to Janice? There are so many controversial areas, and we can't make a major issue out of everything. We are only going to be able to win so many battles so we must choose which battles are important enough to fight.

MAJORS AND MINORS

If you asked your preteen or teen, "What five things do you think are most important to your mom and dad?" what would the answer be? Would these five issues match your own list? Or have you been majoring on the minors?

Each family's list of majors and minors will be a little different. The goal is not to have identical lists, but for the family to decide what is most important.

For us, the majors are our teens' morals and values, their attitude and relationship toward God, honesty, and their peers (Are they willing to stand alone in the midst of peer pressure?). Yet as our boys entered the teen years they daily heard me stressing clothes, rooms, music, grooming, hair styles, and neatness!

It's not that these minors are not issues to be considered and worked through, but in our house minor areas used to become major irritations. If you want to do more than just survive your child's teenage years, you need to major on the majors and minor on the minors. Dave and I have learned to be willing to flex in those areas that are not moral issues. Is it a biblical absolute like lying or premarital sex? Is it really a moral issue or just our personal preference?

To help us determine if the issue is a major or a minor, we've found the following exercise helpful. Draw a similar graph to that in exercise 6, leaving blanks to fill in with your own issues and answers.

One question summarizes this exercise for us if we have to make a quick decision: Is this a moral issue?

Sex before marriage is a moral issue and cannot be negotiated. On the other hand, parents' adversion to long hair stems from their own opinions and biases. Long hair is negotiable, and parents and teens can probably work out a compromise.

We have found it beneficial to work through four steps with our adolescents when we are talking about negotiable issues:

1. Let your preteen or teen summarize what he or she wants.

     Joel: I want to let my hair grow for soccer season. All the other guys on the team have long hair.

2. Summarize what you want.

     Claudia and Dave: We want Joel to be neat. We want him to have a conservative haircut for college interviews.

3. Propose alternatives after you have discussed points 1 and 2.

     a. Let hair grow long.
     b. Keep hair short.
     c. Get a long wig for soccer games.

EXERCISE 6

Majors and Minors[*]

1. Write the issue in question.	Long hair	Sex before marriage
2. Is this an opinion? (a conclusion based on my own feelings or attitudes) We can negotiate.	Yes, I don't like long hair on boys	More than an opinion
3. Is this a bias? (a conclusion based on a teaching, prejudice, or attitude of a certain group) We can negotiate.	Some teach that long hair is a sign of rebellion	More than a bias
4. Is this a conviction? (God's direct teaching as revealed in Scripture or the character of Christ) Then this is a major. Here we can't negotiate.	Many men had long hair in the Bible. Does not appear to be a moral issue Negotiable	This is a conviction. God's word teaches against it: 1 Thess. 4:2 1 Corinth. 6:18 Non-negotiable

4. Work out a compromise.

> Let Joel have long hair, but he must keep it clean and well groomed. Joel will get a haircut after soccer season and before college interviews.

When you're wearing the referee hat in your family, don't hang onto your taboos, and don't make *compromise* a dirty word in your home. We suggest that you learn to major on the majors and minor on the minors.

A letter from Jarrett during his first year in college showed us that he had adopted this philosophy as his own:

> At ROTC this morning, they told me my hair was too long. What are they doing to me? First they made me march; then they are taking up all my weekends, and now, now they want me to get my hair cut like a, a, a...like someone in the Army. Who do they think I am? An ROTC cadet or something?
>
> I asked my commanding officer, "Is it a moral issue?" I soon found out that the Army is not a loving parent and will not compromise in order to insure a wholesome relationship!

In this letter Jarrett was telling Dave and me that he appreciated the standards we had set in our home so much that he was using them to evaluate his own decisions. That was our goal all along.

Let's consider several areas that we have chosen as minors, which tend to cause parent-teen tug-of-wars if they are treated as major issues.

Rooms or Tombs

Do I hear you moaning? Is it true that children can be born neat? (Believe it or not, we've scored two out of three!) Some of us, however, will be able to identify with the mom who said, "I've tried everything from punishment to bribes, but my son's room would still turn a respectable pack rat's stomach."

What can you do? Start by asking yourself, "Is the state of affairs in my child's room a major or a minor?" If your middle name is Heloise, then it is most likely a major; but just as likely it is about forty-fifth on your teen's priority list.

I know the Scripture verse, "Let everything be done decently and in order" could include the tombs that teenagers call rooms. So we decided to try to solve this problem with five approaches, which have met with some measure of success.

Tips for Trying

1. Rewards and Bribes

Make your preteen's allowance based on the condition of his or her room. This worked for a short time, but it required mom to be disciplined too because what isn't inspected will not be accomplished.

One mom gave this challenge to her twelve-year-old daughter who desperately wanted contact lenses: "When you keep your room neat for one month, you have proven you are responsible and old enough for contact lenses."

In case you are worried that you are bribing your child, remember the seals, candy, and special favors teachers give to students who perform well in class. There it's called "positive reinforcement."

2. Humor

Hang a sign by the phone that says on one side: "As I today through your room went walking, I saw that it was O.K. for phone talking." On the other side say: "Today your room did not pass—so no phoning today—Alas! Alas!"

I make no claim to poetic talent but the idea worked, at least with Jarrett who loved that communication medium called the telephone. Joel couldn't have cared less, so limiting the use of the phone was useless with him. Kids may tease you about your silly notes, but they really enjoy them. Think how often they pass them at school!

3. Birthday Box
Put teen's room in his or her birthday box at thirteen as a responsibility (chapter 10).

4. Negotiation
One friend approached her son and said, "Rick, what can we do to make your room work for you?"

Since Rick didn't like his present desk (which went great with the room decor), he studied on the bed, with messy results. The first thing he wanted was a drafting board desk. With this one change, his study habits changed; after all, it's harder to fall asleep at a drafting board than on a bed! Also, they added shelves to his closet and made a place for his hiking boots, sleeping bag, and other camping gear and sports equipment. With things more organized, Rick is doing a much better job of keeping his room clean.

Dave and I thought this was such a clever approach that we tried it with Joel and Jonathan. When Jarrett left for college, Joel inherited his desk and a four-drawer file cabinet. As a high school junior, he was then equipped to look studious. He spent days getting his room and belongings organized, for the first time in his sixteen years. We also put more shelves in his closet and some nails on which he could hang backpacks and other items with handles. Joel did not become a super housekeeper, but we did see remarkable improvement.

5. If nothing works, close the door!
There are times when this is the best approach unless we want to make a clean room a major issue, which will result in a major battle.

Let us assure you, almost everyone has those "closed door days" too. Our teens have moments when their rooms are neat and in order, but not as often as I would like. We encourage neatness but it is not an Arp major!

A View from the Inside

I questioned our teens so I could understand better how they viewed the whole subject of rooms. The following conversation will show you I still struggle in this area.

Mom: "How would you describe your room?"

Teen: "But mom, I picked up my clothes!"

Mom: "How do you like your room?"

Teen: "Cool! Fantastic!"

Mom: "I mean the condition of it. How you keep it."

Teen: "Oh, it's a mess. But that's why it's so cool and fantastic!"

One teen described her ideal room this way: "It's a place that is all yours—where you can shut the door and be alone with your own thoughts. Sometimes my thoughts are jumbled and so my room is too. Sometimes an unmade bed is part of the picture. That's because a cozy nest of blankets and a pillow feel good when you study and eat pretzels on the bed."

Different Perspectives

It's obvious that parents and preteens view kids' rooms from two completely different perspectives. If you aspire to a *House Beautiful* home, then let me give a word of warning. Little children love for mom to "redo" their room with cute toy soldier wallpaper, and your preteen may still enjoy redecorating with you, so now's the ideal time to redo your son's or daughter's room. If you wait until the teen years, you will have to consider things from the teenager's perspective.

I remember getting a brand new room when I was thirteen. My mother let me choose the wallpaper and carpet and even make the curtains. I chose pink and gray, not a great color combination, but my parents allowed me the privilege of choice.

One mom wrote, "Our son has chosen to decorate his room in what can only be termed as 'Early Grotesque.' He has red walls, a red carpet, black drapes, and a fake animal skin spread. Mobiles attack you, posters affront you, anything that takes his fancy we allow. Know why? It's his room, and he's the one who has to live with it. Because it is his own, we have found he would just as soon have friends over as go out, and that means less worry for us. I overheard one kid say, 'Gosh, your parents are great. I wish mine would let me fix my room up!' When you give a little, you get a lot!"

Some young teens do not have the confidence to go it alone. One mother told her thirteen year old that she could decorate her room in any color and style she wanted as long as it was within their budget. The girl shopped and shopped but could not decide what to choose, so she asked mom to help.

Grooming

How is a mom to motivate her preteen to comb his hair, brush his teeth, and be respectably clean? These are not called the groady years for nothing! One answer is to wait. In a matter of months he or she will probably be obsessed with what he is now trying to avoid.

One friend commented, "I still cannot believe it has happened! Six months ago it took a state of war to get my daughter to wash her hair. She seemed not even to notice the grease that looked ready to drip onto her collar.

"Now she has done a total flip-flop! Last night she washed her hair without being asked and rolled it in curlers. This morning she wet her brush, combed out some of the curls, and then recurled them with the curling iron! Now I'm not sure which is better, the greasies or the hair obsession. At least with the greasies I got to use the bathroom sometimes!"

A frequent controversy between parents and young girls is makeup. Often preteens see makeup as a symbol of maturity. They use an eyebrow pencil and mascara as if they were dressing for Halloween. Sometimes this is just a lack of skill; other times it's deliberate. Have you established some guidelines at your house?

One of the mothers in a support group shared her experience: "When my daughters were eleven and twelve, they became very interested in makeup. This seemed too young to me, but rather than allow this to become a 'major,' I agreed to teach them how to use makeup to achieve a natural look. I praised them when they were able to apply a little eyeshadow expertly.

"But would you believe it? Before long they lost interest. Now that they're older, I'm the one who asks them to put a dab of color on their cheeks."

Often teaching a preteen to use makeup properly will solve problems that might develop later. If you do not use much makeup yourself, you might both have your color analyzed. Most analysts will suggest proper makeup to go with your particular skin color and the color coordinates that match your skin. If you ask the analyst, she will probably also show the preteen how to apply makeup properly.

Fads Are for Driving Moms Wild!

Do you remember wearing varsity sweaters, several sizes too big, which were wonderful because they belonged to that special guy? Or starched petticoats, three at least, to make your skirts stand out? Are today's styles really any worse than those of other generations?

In the recent past, teens in our neighborhood have adopted these fads:

1. Sweatbands and bandannas around the head
2. Star and butterfly stickers on the cheeks
3. Hair pulled back on one side and drooping on the other
4. The same shirt with a horse over the heart worn five days in a row
5. Bright pink knit gloves without the fingers
6. T-shirts with the sleeves and bottoms cut off
7. Double pierced ears with one loop earring and one stud

8. Army fatigues
9. Muscle shirts (shirts that are sleeveless or have had the sleeves cut out to show off the muscles)

Do I like these fads? What do you think? I'm over thirty-nine and think the starched petticoats we wore in the 1950s were much more sensible.

The parents of one teen would not let her cut her hair or wear pants because of religious convictions. What did this teenager do? Each morning she went to her friend's house before school and changed from her skirt into her jeans that she hid there. Each week she snipped off a few locks of hair, so gradually her hair got shorter and shorter.

One mother took the opposite approach. "Unless the kid shows a tendency to go berserk or way overboard," she advised, "let them choose for themselves. They will make mistakes, but at least they cannot say, 'My parents made me wear this junk.'"

I'm not sure we would all be willing to go quite that far, but I'm convinced that if you give a little on dress and hair, your preteen or teen will be more apt to respond in the major areas.

One friend told me that in her daughter's early teen years, she bought all her clothes on the street near a local university where she could find clothes mod enough for her taste. One day the daughter, Ginny, joined her mother for a luncheon at a very exclusive private club. All the women and their daughters were dressed conservatively.

My friend told me later, "The only way to describe Ginny's garb was that she looked like a gypsy!"

Did this bother my friend? Would it bother you? When my friend asked herself why she was upset, she had to admit, "It's my pride. I was scared by that age-old worry, 'What will other people think of my daughter?'"

The better question, she knew, was: Is this a moral issue? "No, it isn't," she decided.

This guideline works for most mothers, except in the rare instances when a young person's dress really hurts the teen or someone else. Susan told the women in her support group of just such an experience. Her daughter, Wendy, began to show some interest in clothes when she was eleven, but her taste left much to be desired, so Susan was constantly advising her to change a blouse or skirt so her outfit would match.

Finally Wendy erupted. "I've had enough of your taste, Mom," she asserted. "I want to choose my own clothes."

In exasperation, Susan relented. Wendy went to school with her clothes mismatched and unironed and her hair disheveled. Her mom bit her tongue and let her go. After two weeks, Wendy's teacher called and asked her mom to come in for a consultation.

As soon as Susan sat down, the teacher observed, "You're so nicely dressed. Why doesn't Wendy dress nicely?" The teacher went on to explain that Wendy alienated herself from the other kids by dressing so oddly.

That did it. Susan told Wendy, "You may call the shots on your dress only when you begin to show the ability to dress neatly."

According to Susan, here's the regime that she instituted: "First, I got her a short hairstyle that required no talent to keep, only that she had to comb her hair! Wendy could pick her clothes in the morning, but I had to approve them before she left for school. I agreed to iron for her for one more year, but she was to iron occasionally and take over after that. After three years, this is still a concern, but Wendy has shown much improvement. She'll never be a fashion designer, but she is learning to use taste in her preferences."

Music: Bach or Rock

If your teen is in a total Christian environment, complete with Christian school and friends, the most popular songs in their peer group may be sung by Amy Grant and Evie. Perhaps music is not an issue at your house. But many parents have children who are in secular schools with secular friends.

As the Arp family moved into the teen scene, it became obvious that our blooming adolescents had an interest in new forms of music. Their favorite song, "Help, I Need Somebody," expressed my feeling of inadequacy so I began to poll other moms with older teens who seemed to be doing great. Never overlook the potential gold mine of information and experience from other families who are a few years farther down the road than you are.

After gathering information, Dave and I came up with the following guidelines for the early teen years. As our guys matured and became older, more freedom was given to them in this area.

Our guidelines in the beginning (ages eleven-thirteen) were these:

1. Before school play Christian music.
2. Before bed at night play Christian music.
3. After school no music until homework is completed or at least one hour has been spent on it.
4. On Sunday let rock rest (and Mom's ears too!) and play Christian music.

Our music guidelines worked much of the time. With Joel, we actually wrote out a music contract, which he signed. This helped to spell it out and aided enforcement.

A Word of Caution

This worked for us with Joel, but one dad who read about this contract said his son's response would have been, "Dad, gag me with a Bill Gaither record, but don't ask me to sign that!" I would not recommend using this approach with older adolescents or with kids who are already choosing their own music. Our teens are active in sports, scouting, and many other things so there is not a lot of listening time available to them. Music has not become a major in our home.

Monitor Different Music Groups

Over the years we have monitored the different music groups that our teens listen to. "Are they Christian?" is not

MUSIC CONTRACT BETWEEN JOEL ARP
AND PARENTS

I hereby agree to the following:
1. Before school I will play only Christian music.
2. After school I may play my choice of music after completing one hour of homework.
3. After 8:00 P.M. I will play Christian music.
4. After Jonathan is in bed I will use earphones.
5. At 9:30 P.M. all music will be off.
6. On Sunday I will play only Christian music.

If this contact is broken, I agree to the following:
First offense: No radio or recorder for 24 hours.
Second offense: No radio or recorder for 48 hours.
Third offense: No radio or recorder for 96 hours.

Signed _____
Date _____

our guideline. Personally we believe that restricting a teen only to Christian music makes no more sense than to restrict ourselves to Christian art and Christian books. We do consider groups like Black Sabbath and KISS, which are satanic and blaspheme God in their lyrics or when their records are played backwards, as X-rated.

Since most preteens and teens find it hard to accept a parent's assessment that a group is bad, I polled the Arp teens and here is their advice: "Listen to the lyrics with your preteen. What do the lyrics say? Don't just limit this exercise to rock music. Country music may be more appealing to adults, but some of the lyrics are really immoral. And don't overlook the videos on Music Television (MTV); take the same approach for it."

When Jarrett was fifteen and had proven he could choose his own music with discrimination, we allowed him complete freedom. Did he disappoint his parents? No, he actually became more selective in his choices. Joel, who at thirteen needed firm guidelines for music, had established good values by fifteen. Jonathan set his own standards at the age of twelve. *What do the lyrics say?* he asked himself. To him, the beat was the minor and the words, the major.

From time to time we sit down with our teens, listen to their music, and talk about the lyrics. This has proven to be a good time of communication and teaching as we evaluate the music message together.

I am not saying that there should be complete freedom in music selection, nor that music is never a problem to be dealt with. I am saying that in our experience, by giving in a little, we have achieved a good balance, avoided war, and gained a lot of working capital. We buy Christian tapes and records for our teens, but we let them support their own rock habit.

On his radio program, *Focus on the Family*, Dr. James Dobson said he has compromised in his own home and allowed his sixteen-year-old daughter to listen, within limits, to the secular music of her age. Giving a little in this area, he suggested, can help avoid rebellion in other areas like drugs and sex. Most adolescents have a desire to control their own lives, Dr. Dobson added, and sometimes we strip them of this control just when they most yearn for it. In summary, he challenged parents not to be too legalistic with young teens.

The Saga of the Double-Pierced Ears

Julie came home from the school trip with double-pierced ears. Her parents were furious, shocked, and hurt that their fourteen year old would do this without permission. What would their friends think of their daughter, who to this point had been conservative in her appearance?

After the big explosion Julie was given two alternatives: let the second hole in her ears disappear or give up her own private phone. With a big smile she surrendered her phone! Julie's mother described the situation, "Not only does she still have those double-pierced ears, but now I spend all my time answering her phone calls and hollering up the stairs. Of course she can't hear me because her door is closed and that ghetto blaster is blaring away. I'm asking myself, who is being punished? Are two little holes in her ears major enough to allow so much tension in our relationship?"

Many times we moms find ourselves in a major blowup about a minor issue. Before we know what has happened, we're caught in a struggle we wish we had allowed to pass by. Again, we should stop long enough to ask ourselves, "Is this a moral issue?" If it is, then it should be a major in our families!

NOW IT'S YOUR TURN

Take time now to fill in exercise 7. It's great to read what others have done in similar experiences, but the final decision as to which areas are minor and which are major is yours. Don't make these decisions lightly. You might want to discuss some of the issues with your husband, since you will have to agree on how to handle them. Be sure you don't wait until the problems arise. If you do, you'll be caught in the emotion of the moment.

"I never promised you a rose garden" could be the theme song for both parents and teenagers. Parents must somehow cope with embryo-adults struggling through dramatic physical changes, identity formation, feelings of inferiority, the need to conform, and wild emotional upheavals. Add to these influences the issue of living a Christian life in a sometimes pagan environment and we can see that our teens do not need our hassling them over minor issues. Their relationship with God and withstanding peer pressure are the real majors. Let's save our ammunition for the important battles yet to come.

EXERCISE 7

Dealing With The Minors

I. List five areas that you feel are (or should be) minor issues.

    1.

    2.

    3.

    4.

    5.

II. Relate one situation where you created a major battle over a minor issue.

III. What minor area is creating tension in your home right now?

IV. What can you do to reduce friction in this area this week? Example: If it is your preteen's room, you could close the door.

Chapter Eight

MAJORING ON THE MAJORS

Remember when keys fascinated your child? Our boys were especially intrigued by keys when we lived in Austria where every door was locked. Most apartment houses were surrounded by fences with locked gates, all front doors automatically locked when they closed, and all bedroom doors had locks and keys. In Austria, you had to have keys.

One day when I was returning from the grocery store, I found a strange set of keys lying on the ground beside the front stairs. At dinner that night, I held up the keys and asked, "Does anyone recognize these or know whose they are?"

All three boys answered an immediate "No!"

The next Sunday our pastor announced that the church keys were missing. His description of the keys matched the ones I had found. Our family had the hot goods! I even had a good idea who was guilty.

A couple of weeks before, Jarrett had missed church. When I had asked him why, he had replied, "Oh, Mom, Tobias and I got into a long conversation about the Lord, and we went into Pastor Preston's study to finish our conversation. He's real interested and had lots of questions about Christianity."

How could I argue with a story like that? Our thirteen-year-old son, like his parents, had wanted to share his faith.

Now, two weeks later, my pride turned sour. Dave and I had tried to major on the majors and to ignore the minors. Still Jarrett had lied and stolen, and from the church at that.

That afternoon Dave and I confronted Jarrett.

"We didn't mean any harm," he replied. "We didn't

even know what the keys were to. I really did talk to Tobias about the Lord."

"What do you think the next step is, Jarrett?" Dave asked.

"Give 'em back," he answered reluctantly.

We called Pastor Preston and asked if we could come over to his apartment for a few minutes. Soon after we arrived, Jarrett handed him the keys, told him the whole story, and admitted, "Pastor, I was wrong. Will you forgive me?"

Dave and I will always be grateful for our pastor's wise response. "Jarrett, I do forgive you. When I was growing up, I did some really dumb things, even dumber than taking church keys. But I didn't have the guts to go back and 'fess up. I really respect you for what you have just done."

Dave and I had again been caught off guard by one of Jarrett's capers. Stealing church keys certainly was not part of our plan for Jarrett's thirteenth year. Can parents really set goals for their children?

DESIRES VERSUS GOALS

How often do most parents set goals for their children? It frequently begins with the moment we first hold our babies in the hospital and ask ourselves, "What is this tiny infant's future?" While such goal setting is impromptu, these goals are often firmly set in parents' minds.

Is it realistic, however, to set goals for another person? A goal must be something I alone can achieve. I can set a goal of getting up at six o'clock each morning. It's up to me to get up, and if I want to achieve this goal badly enough, I can do it. Now if I set a goal for Jonathan to get up at 6:00 A.M., that's a horse of a different color!

It is much more realistic to talk about our desires for our children and what we would like to see happen in their lives, realizing that goal setting is personal. We can only alter and affect our own attitudes and actions.

So how can we influence our preteens' lives? In this

chapter we will look together at three areas of major concern: our teen's relationship to his peer group, to others, such as friends and teachers, and to God. In each of these areas we will talk about real situations that have been faced and offer some potential ways of dealing with these problems. There are no definite answers, just approaches, which we hope will encourage you to major on the majors creatively.

TEEN'S RELATIONSHIP TO PEER GROUP

Many teens will admit that their hardest struggle is against peer pressure. One of the seven intuitive goals the Strommens identified was "the broadening of one's social base by having learned to make friends and maintain them." What teen wants to antagonize his or her peers? To be different? Teens want to be carbon copies of each other in speech, dress, and tastes, such as for music.

"Our offspring's urge to conform usually sharpens during the preteen and early teenage years," says Dr. Bruce Narramore in *Adolescence Is Not an Illness*. "Their susceptibility to peer pressure then peaks around middle adolescence, and begins a gradual decline. In spite of the potentially negative influence of peer pressure, the process behind it is entirely natural and God-given. Our teenagers are susceptible to their friends' influence because they are in the process of weaning themselves from us and learning to think for themselves. In a sense, our teenagers are going from one form of dependency, parental, to another form of dependency, peer, on their way to constructive self-reliance."[1]

Psychologists say this is normal and that it too shall pass away. But when it seems to be the all-pervading influence in your teen's life, it is scary. Consider these situations:

SITUATION 1: Pressure in Girl-Boy Relationships
One young teen received the following letter from a friend, who also happened to be his girlfriend's brother, en-

couraging him to "get with it" physically with his girl.

Dear Friend,

If I had a girlfriend I would not let this happen! You're not getting anywhere (holding hands, etc.). Get that shyness away when you're around my sister.

I say this because it seems that when you're around other girls, you're not at all shy! Could you tell me why?

Well, okay, it's not all your fault. I've told her off too. If I were my sister, I would have dropped you long ago but don't worry, she won't. Here are some tips for you.

1. Hold hands (openly)
2. Kiss
3. Hug (openly)
4. Talk to each other

Your Friend

P.S. Don't kill me!

As teens grow older the pressure in boy-girl relationships gets stronger. Dealing with a note like the above is simple in comparison with being in a group where most of the other couples are already sleeping together. How can a parent help in the middle of this kind of peer pressure? How can we prepare our preteens for what's just up the road?

One tool for preparing for peer pressure is the book *Dare to Be Different* by Fred Hartley (published by Scripture Press). Dave has taken our boys individually out to breakfast one morning a week for six weeks (since the book breaks easily into six sections) and discussed the book with each of them. If your husband does not wish to do this, or you are the mother of girls, mom and preteen can go out for breakfast.

A book which warns older teen girls against the problems of promiscuous sex is *Just Like Ice Cream* by Lissa Johnson.

Teens can survive peer pressure much better when they

know what they believe and have decided beforehand on their standards of action. However, even with this advance preparation, they will still slip at times. If parents are majoring on the majors, we realize that we are building for the future and not expecting perfection today.

SITUATION 2: Pressure to Change Beliefs

It didn't take long for Jarrett to let off steam one day when he came home from school. "Boy, did I get burned today! I got into a discussion with Jason about creation versus evolution, and he made me look stupid and ridiculous! I still believe I am right, but I guess you just can't defend creation."

Who likes to be made fun of or to be considered different? Our preteens will soon have to face situations like the above or comments such as these, "Surely you don't actually believe the Bible. Everyone knows it's full of contradictions!" "Christianity is an outdated religion." "There are no absolutes—just do what feels good to you." How can we help our children combat such statements?

First, it is important to identify with adolescents in their struggles and give them space to question and search for the truth. We can also offer practical help. Here are some ways we helped Jarrett, our budding creation scientist:

1. We provided reference material on creation versus evolution that he could study.

2. We set up an appointment for Jarrett to talk with Dr. Joseph Dillow, who is an expert in this area. He had a chance to repeat Jason's questions and learn biblical responses.

3. We offered to have a rap session in our home for our teen and his friends. (He did not take us up on this offer.)

4. Along with Jarrett, we watched an excellent slide show on the Bible and science, which Dr. Dillow had put together, and discussed the show afterward. (You might also wish to read together *What High School Students Should Know about Evolution* by Kenneth Taylor.)

What were the results of our efforts? Let's drop in on a conversation several months later.

"Mom, you won't believe it! One night on the ski team trip we had a fantastic debate about creation versus evolution. It was nine for evolution and one—me—for creation. But in the end, Jason said, 'Gee, we have to admit, your arguments are just as logical as ours!' "

Three years later, Jarrett, as a senior in high school, was brave enough to challenge the head of a university science department in front of two hundred fellow students about the same issue. The professor was impressed enough to look up this student after the lecture and compliment Jarrett on his questions.

Whatever the point of peer pressure, we can help our teens explore the subject. Sometimes they are open to our suggestions; other times outside resources are necessary.

SITUATION 3: Pressure to Slip Out at Night

Quite a few parents experience a middle-of-the-night trauma when they wake up and find their teens have sneaked out of the house. Sometimes teens get caught by the parent or, even worse, by the police.

Judy slipped out of the house the first time one night when her best friend, Susie, was spending the night. Their plan? To "roll" (or "teepee") some yard. One might define "rolling" as a form of art in which trees and mailboxes are decorated with toilet paper. The girls returned without Judy's parents seeing them.

The next time Judy tried this caper, she was not so lucky. She and some friends decided to drive to an old house everyone said was haunted. After they arrived, one boy suggested, "We need a souvenir. Why don't we take the mailbox? Bet witches don't get any mail."

Everyone agreed, and they began to pull and tug on the mailbox. No one saw the blue lights of the police car when it approached.

The four teens had been looking for excitement but not

a ride in the patrol car to the juvenile detention center or being locked in cells. Two long hours later, Judy and her friends were released to their parents. "Honestly, we didn't know anyone lived in that house," Judy told her parents as they drove home. "We just wanted to have fun. I'm sorry. I'll never, never slip out again."

Judy's parents managed to remain calm and simply said, "We're glad you're O.K. and not hurt. We'll discuss it in the morning and work out the consequences."

The next morning the parents of the four teens met together. First, they made sure all the facts were correct. Yes, the house was known as the haunted house, as the teens had claimed. Yes, lots of kids had vandalized it, but that was no excuse. An old woman lived in the house, and her life had been made very unpleasant by all the pranks.

Together the parents agreed upon the teens' punishment. All four teens would apologize to the woman and then spend the next Saturday mowing her yard and helping her with other housework.

Did the teens learn their lesson? Yes. Did they ever slip out again at night? We don't think so.

These parents adopted the advice in that famous Gilbert and Sullivan opera *The Mikado,* "Let the punishment fit the crime."

SITUATION 4: Pressure to Drink

"My friends won't come!" Ruth protested to her mother. "The party won't be any fun. Anyway, if they knew I wasn't going to have anything to drink, they'd bring their own."

Someday you, like Corrie, Ruth's mother, may be asked to allow liquor at your teen's party. Ruth's mother stood firm in her decision, but she allowed Ruth to have the party. Corrie went all out on the food and even found a non-alcoholic drink called "Near Beer."

"Eeee Gad, Mom!" Ruth shrieked when her mother showed her the bottles. "That's worse than Kool Aid!"

The night of the party, Ruth's father stood beside the

bushes at the door to their house. When the first guest arrived, toting a cooler, he asked, "Son, what do you have in the cooler? Could I have a look inside?"

"Oh, it's just some extra ice and pop."

"Well, we've got plenty inside. Why don't you leave your cooler in the car."

That scenario was repeated over and over again.

The next day Ruth told her parents, "The party was a complete disaster! How could you and Dad do this to me?"

Later that night Corrie and her husband, Bill, evaluated the party fiasco and came up with these conclusions:

1. Our daughter hates us and is socially ruined.

2. We have two cases of untouched Near Beer.

3. We have prevented a drinking party.

On top of this, Bill was covered with mosquito bites. But what would have happened if there had been liquor at the party? The possibilities were too scary to think about, the parents decided.

"We'll take a disaster any day," they agreed. Corrie did, however, regret the Near Beer. "It's just an older version of candy cigarettes," she said. "The kids knew it was a foolish substitute."

A year later, that disastrous party had almost been forgotten. Ruth still had many friends, but she had found other ways to entertain them, such as riding on her family's new motorboat. Her father had recently driven Ruth and eleven of her friends in a van for twelve hours to a Christian Youth Congress in Washington, D.C.

What can parents do to offset peer pressure to drink? First, we can get involved as Ruth's parents did. Bill and Corrie say they would have preferred ten days of forced labor to that party, but the experience did help direct their daughter in another direction.

Secondly, we can check on the parties to which our teens are invited. When our boys were in their early teen years, we called the parents before we let them attend a party at a friend's home. "Will there be an adult chaperone?" I always asked. "Will drinks be served or allowed?"

When one mother responded, "Oh, no, I won't be home," Dave and I did not allow Joel to attend. I've heard too many stories about parties that were held when parents were away for the evening or out of town.

Thirdly, you can encourage your teen to get involved in an organization like Students Against Drunk Driving (SADD).

One mom told me how her son, Kurt, and his friends decided to do something positive to counteract the alcohol problem in his high school. They heard that a SADD chapter, which had become inactive, had been a positive influence, so they decided to form a new one. The track coach agreed to be the sponsor, and he and the boys attended some training conferences and began to bring speakers to the school. Soon the chapter had thirty members.

One project their SADD chapter chose to sponsor was an After Prom Party, which kids could attend without the pressure to drink. A couple of weeks before the prom, they placed a wrecked car in front of the school with a sign that read: "Friends don't let friends drive drunk."

SADD suggests that parents and teenagers get together in a unique partnership, which they call a "Contract for Life." The teenager signs a part of this drinking-driver contract, in which he or she pledges: "I agree to call you for advice and/ or transportation at any hour, from any place, if I am ever in a situation where I have had too much to drink or a friend or date who is driving me has had too much to drink."

The parents also sign a pledge in the contract, which reads: "I agree to come and get you at any hour, any place, no questions asked and no argument at that time, or I will pay for a taxi to bring you home safely. I expect we would discuss this issue at a later time.

•123•

"I agree to seek safe, sober transportation home if I am ever in a situation where I have had too much to drink."

(A free copy of this contract or material to start a SADD chapter can be obtained by writing: SADD, Corbin Plaza, Marlboro, Mass. 01752.)

SITUATION 5: Pressure to Take Drugs

One afternoon a professional counselor received a call from the emergency room of a local hospital. "Your son has overdosed on drugs. Could you come immediately?" said the voice on the other end of the line.

The counselor, who often worked with adolescents, had been worried about his middle son ever since his grades began slipping a year earlier. Lately, he had suspected the boy was taking drugs. *Why didn't I confront him with my suspicions?* he wondered as he walked into the hospital. Fortunately the doctors soon assured him that his son was O.K.

Later, when he saw the teenager, the boy admitted, "Gee, Dad, this is the worst thing I've ever done to you and Mom. But I'm glad it happened. I won't do it again."

Even with the boy's promise, we would be naive to assume the next months were easy for these parents. As a counselor, the father knew how many teens make such promises and still end up as addicts. They could have been consumed with guilt, but their comments to me hold wisdom for all parents.

In our work, we have learned that you can't assume responsibility for other people's decisions. Our son is the one who decided to try drugs, not us. We tried not to dwell on the past, forever wondering, "How did this happen?" Instead, we looked to the future. "How can we help him turn this thing around?"

When he came home from the hospital, we did all we could to structure his environment. We had rules, and he had to abide by them. We were the parents, and we did assert our authority. Because we did not carry the guilt for his unwise choices, we were not paralyzed by a sense of failure and consumed with guilt. We were free to help him.

With professional counseling this teenager lived up to his promise. His grades went back up, he graduated from high school, and he is doing extremely well in college.

No matter how dark the situation looks, parents need to focus on the future, as these people did, not on the past. "Where do we go from here?" is the proper question, not "How did this happen?"

Drugs are not a fad, which will soon go out of style or be successfully controlled by law. Wise parents will arm themselves with valid information.

Art Linkletter, whose youngest daughter died when she jumped out of a building during an LSD trip, gives this advice:

> You can't watch your children 24 hours a day. You can try to build a relationship with the child that will form a protective barrier between him and the drug menace. I'm not saying you will succeed; in spite of your best efforts, you may fail. But you will know you've tried—and believe me, this knowledge in itself may save your own sanity.[2]

Linkletter goes on to encourage parents to spend more time with their kids. Be sure to talk and to listen, he advises. "They need to know that you are interested in them, that you trust them, expect the best of them. But don't be complacent, assuming that everything's all right," he adds.[3]

Self-esteem is seen as a contributing factor to drug addiction by many psychologists. "Most researchers in the field—even those who disagree about other matters of causation and treatment—agree that low self-regard is a crucial factor in addiction," say Dr. Harvey Milkman, associate professor of psychology at Metropolitan State College in Denver, and Dr. Stanley Sunderwirth, professor of chemistry and vice-president for academic affairs at the same college. "One way of coping with feelings of worthlessness is to immerse oneself in mood altering behavior."[4]

These two educators also point out that the stigma of being diagnosed as a drug user further decreases the adolescent's sense of self-worth and pushes him or her more firmly into a pattern of socially unacceptable behavior. Frequently this downward spiral results in hospitalization. Research has shown that 60 to 80 percent of all addicts who attempt abstinence fail within six months.

Instead of being petrified by these statistics, parents need to maintain a loving relationship with their child if drug addiction occurs, as one dad did. He was called to pick up his son at the police station and was told, "He's your problem now."

"No, he's not my problem," the dad replied, "he's my son and I love him." That dad was on the right track. He recognized his son's problem and, therefore, sought counseling for the boy, but he continued to love his son unconditionally.

In his book *My Child on Drugs?* Linkletter gives the following signs and signals of drug use:

1. Lack of appetite, especially in a teenage boy
2. Short attention span
3. Slothfulness or lethargy
4. Drowsiness
5. Drunken appearance
6. Loss of memory
7. Impaired judgment
8. Staying away from home for unexplained lengths of time[5]

"A good rule," he adds, "is to be suspicious of any sudden change that is completely out of character for the individual." He also encourages parents to get to know their child's friends, to set loving limits, and to get professional help—before their child becomes another statistic.

(If you would like to read more about teen drug abuse, I particularly recommend two books: *My Child on Drugs?* by Art Linkletter and George Gallup, Jr., and *Tough Love* by Pauline Neff.)

As we help our preteens work through these major pressures in the years ahead, let's remember that today's giant redwood was once a little nut that held its ground!

TEEN'S RELATIONSHIP TO OTHERS

Preteens and teens, particularly girls, can be very catty. They can talk behind one another's backs and hurt one another unintentionally and intentionally. God has asked us to respond with a blessing when we are hurt or insulted. In 1 Peter 3:9, we read: "Do not return evil for evil or reviling for reviling but on the contrary blessing, knowing that you were called to this, that you might inherit a blessing."

It is hard for adults, and even harder for teens, to respond in this way. When hurt, our natural response is to hurt back, when insulted, to insult back. Our teens' lives are full of opportunities to respond with a blessing, but they need our help. Consider the following situations.

SITUATION 1: Responding When the Truth Has Been Misrepresented

Seventh grade Christy sobbed to her mom, "She lied to him about me. I never said that it bugged me when he called. Now he doesn't call and hardly speaks to me. All because of her lie. Oh, I hate her!"

Mom listened to Christy, then tried to identify with her feelings by acknowledging, "It hurts when a friend lets you down. I know how you feel." Once Christy had calmed down and knew mom understood, she was more open for suggestions.

Too often we begin dishing out advice before our teen has finished explaining the problem. Have you ever been guilty of giving a pious response? Have you ever said something such as, "Christians are supposed to love each other" or, "You have got to live your faith." No wonder we get responses like, "Mom, you just don't listen. You don't understand at all!"

What is a better way to proceed? The first important step for Christy's mom was simply to listen and try to identify Christy's feelings. She gave her daughter time to cool down. Then she asked Christy what she might do tomorrow at school to give her friend a blessing and suggested saying something kind and positive to her. Christy wasn't sure she could do that, but she agreed to give her a smile. A smile is a beginning for all of us.

SITUATION 2: Responding to One in Authority, Even When He or She Is Wrong

This is hard for an adult and an extra big order for a teen. The teacher had not only sworn at Matt, but he had also ridiculed his faith in God in front of the whole class! Sometimes our teens do respond correctly and this was one of them. Matt had kept his cool and had even forgiven the teacher before the end of the period. A big help was the fact that the teacher, realizing he was wrong, had asked for forgiveness.

When our teens give the right response, we can help to reinforce and support it. Matt's mother called the teacher and invited him to dinner. They, as a family, reached out to him and began to build a relationship with him, a real picture of giving a blessing for an insult! They continued to take an interest in him and his problems, and what was the result? Before many months had passed, the teacher made a commitment to Christ, and Matt's response was, "Gee, Mom, this is worse than before! Now at school I'm his pet. I'd much rather be his enemy than his pet!"

Well, you can't win them all! I believe deep down Matt

saw the real issues and, despite his comments, learned the value of responding in the right way.

TEEN'S RELATIONSHIP TO GOD

If I were asked, "What is the thing that you would most like for your teen?" I would answer, "I want my teen to have a relationship with Christ." (Again, we are talking about one of those seven goals an adolescent intuitively seeks: "The sense of knowing 'who I am,' of being recognized as a significant person.") For Dave and me, our ultimate identities and significance come from our relationship to God as his children.

As our boys reached the teenage years, we began to realize they needed two special friends, adults besides ourselves as role models and Christian friends. If you have a vital youth group in your church, or groups like Young Life and Student Venture at your local schools, count yourself blessed. When Jarrett and Joel were young teens, we lived in Austria where Christians were a small minority. Consider these situations.

SITUATION 1: No Christian Youth Group
"Mom, how would you like to be the only thirteen year old in the church and have no Sunday school class?" Jarrett complained to me one Sunday morning when we were living in Vienna. "Would you be excited to go to church, Mom, if you were in my shoes?"

No, I admitted to myself. I might even choose to be a Sunday school dropout, which is what my son was considering.

I briefly thought about lecturing on how God deserves our faithfulness even if we are bored to tears. After all, Joseph did not have Christian friends in Egypt, I could remind Jarrett. I'd learned long ago, however, that this approach doesn't work.

Instead I decided to help Jarrett create a group of his own. With our pastor's blessings, Dave and I started an event that became known as "Friday Pancakes." Every other Friday, Jarrett could invite his friends from school to come to our house for pancakes. (Once this group was established, we often substituted popcorn for pancakes. It was not so sticky, I found, and much, much simpler.)

We asked some young adults, who went to our church and related well to teens, to take turns leading the pancake parties. Skits, table tennis, video movies, and short talks on how God relates to a teenager's world were among the activities.

At first both Dave and I were ill at ease with this age group. But remember this is a major in our family, so we really worked on relating to these boys and girls. Now, years later, we both enjoy being with teens; in fact, they are some of the best people we know.

SITUATION 2: No Christian Friends at School

Have you ever tried to give two birthday parties each year for each child? Of course not. However, a friend of mine held duplicate birthday parties for her two preteen daughters for two years, with a purpose behind her madness.

Both daughters had friends at their church, which was half an hour's drive from their home, but the girls at church attended different schools. Sunday morning was the only time they were together.

To compensate, my friend Linda began birthday slumber parties. On each of the girl's birthdays, they entertained their friends from church at one "slumberless party" and their friends from school at another. The extra work and late nights were worth it to Linda since her daughters had close Christian friends during these important formative years.

Dr. Bruce Narramore advises parents to try to get their children in a good homogeneous peer group. Cultivate their friends and have an open home policy, he advises. Spend the extra gas and give rides to soccer, scouts, and youth group. He adds, "Parents who know and like their adolescent's friends and are comfortable having them around are much less likely to have problems with negative peer influence."[6]

It's so easy to get discouraged when you hear of other situations where there are so many Christian activities for teens. *If only we lived there and had these activities for our teens*, you think. However, no one has to sit back and sulk because parents can get involved, as Dr. Narramore suggests. We must remember, nevertheless, that we are still partly spectators of our children's spiritual growth.

FROM DIRECTOR TO SPECTATOR

We can do all we can do outwardly, but it is only God who can motivate our teens from within. Internalizing their faith is hard, for them and for us, as we stand by and watch them doubt and question. One mom in a support group expressed her fear this way:

If I had grown up in a Christian home, perhaps it would be easier to know what is "normal" for my teens to go through in internalizing their faith. Both my husband and I became Christians at age twenty and were born running. We see our teens questioning, searching, doubting, and making statements like, "I'm not interested in all this religious stuff." "I want to run my own life."

We see them having an internal war within, struggling with the world and the desire to be popular and accepted. It's like they're walking on a tightrope, balancing precariously between commitment to the Lord and commitment to the lifestyle of their peers. One week they are leaning toward the world. The next week they are in tears saying that they have gone away from the

Lord and want to come back. Or worse yet, they seem hostile and indifferent.

A young friend in her twenties tells me that this is all so normal. And I think, "Oh, good—it's normal!" but my stomach doesn't understand and it feels like a huge knot that tightens each time a statement of doubt is verbalized. I remember the chill I felt when I first realized that my children can choose *not* to obey God and to turn away from all they have been taught. Of course I knew this, but before I hadn't *felt* it. It comes down to trusting God for what you can't see. I have to do that in every area of their lives, but somehow it is hardest in the spiritual area.

MAKING IT THEIR OWN

Recently I talked to a friend who is a gifted Bible teacher. She was struggling with her teenage daughter. "Why won't Carol let me teach her spiritual truths? I offer and offer and she makes one excuse after another. She's just not interested in things of the Lord and I feel like a failure as a mother. Where did I go wrong?"

If your teen comes to you and says, "Mom, let's study the Bible together," count yourself extremely fortunate. You are an exception. But aren't we supposed to train our children and doesn't that include teaching them God's Word? Yes, but the moments for parent-child teaching become more infrequent as our kids progress through adolescence.

In the early childhood years, we read Bible stories and taught them Bible verses. Then in the primary grades, we made charts and quiet time notebooks. We sent boxes to missionaries and taught them about giving to others. In the preteen and teen years, our role once again changes.

Now we lead by example, by praying for them and by allowing them the freedom to internalize their faith, to go from outward standards that they must obey to inner convictions that are their own.

FREEDOM TO CHOOSE

A teen is not free to choose God's way as his own until he is given the choice. A belief must be chosen freely from a variety of alternatives, say psychologists like Lawrence Kohlberg. What if he or she makes the wrong choice? Believe me that's not as scary as if he is never given the opportunity to choose. What if your child leaves home equipped only with a habit of conforming to your standards?

He enters a new world, no longer surrounded by your influence, but without well worked through convictions of his own. That can spell confusion and heartache in terms of experimentation and trying to sift through all kinds of new philosophies. How much better it is to form convictions while still at home.

STANDARDS TO CONVICTIONS

In our home we have worked at shifting the responsibility for our teens' walk with the Lord from our shoulders to theirs. Here are some ways we have tried to do this.

Face the issue directly.

At age eleven or twelve we have told our preteen, "You are growing up and very soon you will be a teenager. This is an exciting time in life. It's a time of maturing, a time of questioning, and a time of deciding just who you are and what you believe.

"You'll find yourself questioning things we have taught you and that's O.K. We don't want you to believe the Bible and believe in God just because we told you to. Neither do we want to decide for you. We'll help you along the way, we'll answer your questions and help you find the answers we don't know. Remember, questioning is normal and it's good."

This kind of conversation starts the process of shifting responsibility from our shoulders to theirs, but we still are very much involved in giving input.

Provide good books and tapes.

While our boys were still willing (age eleven-thirteen), we suggested they read some books and listen to particular tapes. At this age the boys loved to go out to breakfast with Dad. (At fourteen or fifteen the same boy may think this activity is dumb.) Some of the books and tapes we used are:

1. *Growing Pains* by Fred Hartley (Power Books, Scripture Press)
2. *Preparing for Adolescence* by Dr. James Dobson (available both as a paperback book and as cassette tapes, Gospel Life)
3. *How to Be Your Own Selfish Pig* by Susan Schaeffer Macaulay (a book of apologetics for teens, which looks at the "gimme myths" of today's society through the magnifying glass of Christian beliefs)

We have also found that preteens love fact books with stories of well-known athletes, stars, and businessmen who are living their Christian beliefs every day, and of Christian preteens and teens who have written books, made archaeological discoveries, and testified in courtrooms about their faith. A preteen quickly realizes, "I am not so alone. There are many other kids and adults who share my Christian faith and withstand peer pressure. I can do it too."

Encourage preteens and teens to ask questions.

Throughout this book you have read the escapades of one Jarrett Arp, our oldest son. Unfortunately, most of the shared incidents have been times when Jarrett tested Dave's and my ability as parents. He's been a great sport to allow me to use these stories in this book. Many of our enjoyable experiences with this special young man will remain in his parents' hearts.

Jarrett has spoken to Moms' Support Groups to give the mothers insight into the teen perspective. The last two ways to guide your young teen in the important area of spiritual growth will come from the "horse's mouth," from this teenager who is about to graduate to adulthood.

One of the major points Jarrett always stresses is "to encourage your preteens and teens to ask questions." He tells the story of a thirteen-year-old girl who attended our church.

"She was involved in Bible studies and youth activities but not strongly committed to the Lord. One day she asked her dad, 'How do I know God exists?' "

"Lucy, how could you ask such a question?" her dad replied. "I've brought you up in a Christian home. How could you ask if God exists?"

To Jarrett, Lucy's question is the most fundamental question man has ever asked, and I agree. Contrast this father's response with the reply Dr. Francis Schaeffer, a well-known evangelical philosopher, gave his daughter, Susan, when she asked the same question, a story Susan relates in her book *How to Be Your Own Selfish Pig*.

> I still remember the quiet, friendly companionship in the atmosphere when my dad finally answered me. "Susan," he said, "those are good questions. I'm glad you've asked them."
>
> What a relief. That dizzy, lonely feeling left me. It was O.K. to ask questions! It was important for me to find out for myself if what I believed was true.
>
> As we talked that night, I discovered that my dad had asked these same questions about God in his own search for answers. Dad opened the door for me into a

new adventure. He said that I didn't have to go through life with a blindfold on my mind to believe in God, merely clinging to hopes and feelings. Neither did I have to throw my beliefs out the window.

If something is true, he explained, you can look at it hard, and think about it, and compare it with other beliefs, and it will stand. It will be reliable.

I decided to do just that.[7]

Jarrett admits, "I asked some questions that really surprised my parents. I was the resident cynic in our house. But my parents always encouraged me to question and helped me to find answers if they didn't feel qualified to respond to my questions. I learned that Christianity is rational and logical; it is not the blind faith some say it is.

"Remember, your teen must have the answers. When you were in high school, a Christian belief undergirded education. Now it's different. Kids face hot issues in high school, like abortion, premarital sex, and evolution versus creation. If you don't answer their questions, someone else will."

Model your faith.

"If you are going to spend your life teaching your children the fundamentals of the Christian faith, make sure you teach them convictions, not contradictions," Jarrett says. "I mean, make sure they see that you live your beliefs. This is the strongest case for your faith.

"For instance, some parents ignore their mistakes when they treat their kids wrong. After all, they're in authority, so they just let it slide. But if my mom had been unjust or lost her temper, she would say, 'I'm sorry, Jarrett. I was wrong.'

"How you handle times like this makes your faith valid to your kids. If you also forgive us when we blow it and love us unconditionally, we know that the faith you are advocating is real."

How to be Your Own Selfish Pig is an excellent resource for teens' questions about God and Christian belief. I recommend you get this book and go through it with your teen as he or she begins the search for a personal faith.

We have considered four initial ways to encourage your child's spiritual growth. In chapter 10, "Countdown to Adulthood," we will talk about helping an older teen to grow in his or her faith.

A Final Word

Now that you have lived through some major difficulties with other parents, I encourage you to return to exercise 6. All of these stories will be useless to you unless you make some decisions right now, before your preteen enters the teenage years. Pick your majors carefully and talk about them with your husband.

Then you and your husband major on the majors. Together answer your adolescent's questions, all of them today, for tomorrow your child may not be asking them. Encourage independent thinking and enjoy the unique character developing before you. Take it from Jarrett and the many other teens in this book: Majoring on the majors not only saves your sanity, it preserves that essential relationship between you and your teen.

PART FOUR

Release: Graduating Kids into Adulthood

Chapter Nine

THE LAUNCHING PAD

Have you ever considered that you should be working yourself out of a job? If you agree with us that the ultimate goal of parenting is to prepare your child to function independently, then you need to begin early to plan for the actual launching from the home pad.

Certainly this big event of turning control over to a young person requires as detailed a countdown as the agenda to propel a rocket into space. Ray Ortland, pastor of a church in California, and his wife Anne put it this way: "It's important that we plan for the time when we'll begin to let go of our children. We need to tell them, 'The day is coming when you're going to leave the house and go off to college, and home may never really be the same to you again. You'll be becoming your own person.' "[1]

The problem with most thinking parents, however, is how to accomplish this formidable task, how to do the actual planning for the great day ahead. A common cop-out is to pray, cross fingers, duck your head, and hope teen time will pass quickly.

A better approach, we believe, is to establish a strong foundation with an adolescent and then begin the process of releasing your child so he or she can become an adult. This step must be done gradually so the principles we have taught from early childhood can become ingrained in the teen.

It's Coming

If we could take a trip into the minds of those who know John and are anticipating the coming transformation, we might hear something like this:

John's mother: "I know it's coming, but I'd rather not think about it."

John's dad: "It's going to cost me a lot more money."

John's teacher: "If we could put them on a desert island for twenty-four months and then pick them up, we could all survive!"

Pizza shop owner: "Couldn't make it financially without them!"

John (age 12): "Can't wait—in three months my life will really begin!"

What's coming that simultaneously causes anxiety, apprehension, and anticipation? It's the birth of a teenager! And this is not without some amount of pain and suffering! One mother wrote, "Why does my almost thirteen year old want to grow up so fast? It's as if she enjoys being miserable. What do I do?"

THE TEENAGE CHALLENGE

One practical tool, called the "Teenage Challenge," is a one-time project first suggested by our friend Phyllis Stanley. We found it so helpful with Jarrett that we made it a family tradition for Joel and Jonathan, who also entered the teenage world through the door of this challenge. There are many others in Moms' Support Groups who have adapted this simple "experience" to make the transition to the teen years a happy new phase of family life.

Let's look again at John and his family. Suppose they had taken the approach characterized by anticipation and preparation instead of apprehension? Their comments would have been:

Mother: "I'm really excited about John's thirteenth birthday. It's a big deal at our house. It's been a lot of work helping him with his Teenage Challenge, but he's really going to make it!"

Dad: "John has worked hard on his Teenage Challenge! Our campout together was a super time of beginning to relate man-to-man. Changes are coming in our family, but we're all excited about them."

The Teenage Challenge, a practical "how-to" for preparing for the teenage years, will make a difference. As a result of this experience, our teens entered their teen years a little less shaky, a little more self-assured, and a little more positive. I might add that we as parents entered this new phase of family life with real hope instead of a sense of impending doom.

What Is the Teenage Challenge?

About six to nine months before their thirteenth birthdays, we told each of our boys, "We want to prepare you for your teen years by giving you a Teenage Challenge. The challenge will include achievement in four different areas: physical, intellectual, spiritual, and practical. We'd like you to think about how you would like to grow in each of these areas. Think of specific exciting projects you could do. Then we will sit down together and write the challenge. If you complete it by your thirteenth birthday, you will receive a reward."

Along with this proposal went an important message, "We are excited! You are getting ready to enter a special time of life. You're on your way to adulthood. We want to help you be ready for this new phase of your life, and this challenge will help you prepare. It is a big deal! You are going to be a teenager! We as your parents are happy about this!"

Positive excitement is contagious, and we want to infect our adolescents with positive attitudes of anticipation, and also give them the gift of advance preparation.

You can be as creative as you and your teen want to be, customizing the challenge to fit your preteen's individual needs and personality. One preteen shows financial irresponsibility, so you decide it would be good for him or her to learn to keep a budget, whereas another preteen has been a certified accountant since age six and has a fatter savings account than you do. A third preteen may need to polish up her swimming skills, whereas her sister at thirteen was a starter on the swim team.

Let me also encourage you to include an activity to increase your child's ability in an area where he or she is particularly talented.

TEENAGE CHALLENGE FOR JONATHAN

I. Physical Goals
   A. Run one mile in under eight minutes.
   B. Learn to play a good game of tennis: work on serve, forehand, and backhand.

II. Intellectual Goals
   A. Read one missionary biography and write a report.

III. Spiritual Goals
   A. Work out your own standards and convictions for your teenage years. Do a Code of Conduct Bible Study and a Study of Proverbs to see God's view of habits such as laziness, pride, cheating, and lying. [These studies can be found in the appendices in Dillow and Arp's *Sanity in the Summertime* (Nashville: Thomas Nelson Publishers, Inc., 1981).]
   B. Memorize Psalm 1.

IV. Practical Goals
   A. Earn $35.00. We will match what you save before your birthday.
   B. Plan and execute an overnight campout with Dad.

Dave and I discussed the Teenage Challenge for each of our boys, wrote down our ideas, and then asked the boys to let us look over their suggestions. Then we took each boy out for lunch to discuss the final document. Allowing your preteen to participate in this challenge is the initial step in making the child responsible for his own life. The steps of this process are outlined in exercise 8.

June is the ideal month to begin, since your preteen has summer vacation in which to complete the challenge. Our two older boys had September birthdays, which were perfect; however, Jonathan's birthday was in March, so we gave him his Teenage Challenge the summer before his thirteenth birthday.

The timing can be flexible, but the key is to allow plenty of time. One mom I know gave her son his challenge two weeks before his birthday. Their house was in chaos for those fourteen days. A last-minute challenge is not recommended, so plan ahead.

When the mile has been run, the campout and book report completed, and every item checked off, both parents and preteen breathe a sigh of relief. Now it's time to celebrate. Here are several suggestions:

1. A special gift is given to the new teen for a job well done. It may be a surprise, or the preteen may have suggested it at the initial luncheon. Some preteens need more motivation than others so it's smart, if possible, to tie the challenge in with a gift they really want. Whatever the gift, the message is, "Congratulations on a job well done. We are proud of you."

2. A special family meal is prepared for the celebration. Pick a menu that your new teen thinks is super and include family and friends if you like. Whatever you do, make your new teen the star for that day.

3. A special certificate is presented to be hung in the teen's room (see illustration 4).

CERTIFICATE OF TEENAGEHOOD

This is to certify that _____
has successfully completed all tests to prove he is prepared to
enter the wonderful and challenging world of a teenager.

OFFICIALLY CERTIFIED THIS ____ DAY OF
_____, 19____

"Trust in the Lord with all your heart,
        And lean not on your own understanding;
        In all your ways acknowledge Him,
        And He shall direct your paths."
                                    Proverbs 3: 5-6

Proud Parents

John Jefferson's Completed Test: 19____
Spiritual: Memorized Philippians 2:3-11
Physical: Ran the mile under eight minutes (7:24)
Mental: Reported on the life of Albert Schweitzer
Practical: Planned and completed an overnight bike hike
          with Dad (94 km)
          Earned $40.00 with own effort

Parents' signatures _____

_____

Teen's signature _____

Illustration 4

The End Is the Beginning

The Teenage Challenge sets the stage for the coming teen years. Two benefits for the parents are:
- It gives a positive emotional start to the teen years.
- It helps the family relate as a team.

The benefits for the preteen include:
- Beginning the teenage years with a sense of accomplishment.
- An increased awareness that the parents realize he or she is growing up.
- Developing comradeship with his or her parents and a realization that they are one team.

When you reach this challenging stage of family life, turn it to your advantage and challenge your soon-to-be teen. Both the adolescent and you will reap many benefits in the years to come.

EXERCISE 8

Steps to Develop a Teenage Challenge

I. Ask your preteen to read chapter 13, "How to Make Your Parents Your Friends," by Jonathan Arp, our youngest son. Ask for an honest opinion of this chapter and listen respectfully to the response.

II. Explain the Teenage Challenge to your preteen and give him or her a photocopy of Jonathan's challenge as an example. Ask your teen to write down the goals he or she would like to set. If your preteen wants your help, spend a couple of hours discussing the goals and projects together.

III. Go out for coffee or lunch with your husband or go to a quiet place by yourself. Look over the list of your preteen's strengths and weaknesses from exercise 2 in chapter 2.

   A. List positive areas you would like to reinforce.

      1.

      2.

      3.

      4.

      5.

B. List areas that you would like to strengthen.

1.

2.

3.

4.

5.

IV. Choose from the above to formulate the Teenage Challenge and write specific goals for these areas:

A. Physical

1.

2.

3.

B. Intellectual

1.

2.

3.

C. Spiritual

1.

2.

3.

D. Practical

1.

2.

3.

V. Evaluate the Teenage Challenge by answering these questions:

A. Is it practical? Have we added too much or too little?

B. Is it programmed for success? Will it stretch our preteen, yet be obtainable? Is it too easy? (If it is, it will not be meaningful.)

C. Is it measurable? Will our preteen know when he has successfully met the requirements? Is there a reasonable time limit?

D. Are the rewards clearly defined?

VI. Parents, make a date with your preteen for lunch or dinner. Compare the preteen's list of goals and projects with the parents' list and work together to combine them, eliminating parts of each list if necessary. Be sure to include items from the adolescent's own list. Be sure not to force your ideas on him or her.

VII. Discuss the reward with your preteen. Would he or she like it to be a surprise? Or does the preteen have some special gift he or she would particularly like?

VIII. Together, sign the document. Again, be sure that the young person accepts each of these projects as his or her own. If the preteen shows any hesitancy over any item, continue discussion and make adjustments until the young person is truly excited and comfortable about the project.

Chapter Ten

COUNTDOWN TO ADULTHOOD

After a successful launch into the teen years, the countdown to adulthood is well underway. The Teenage Challenge project detailed in the last chapter led up to the thirteenth birthday. Now it's time for the Birthday Boxes, an ongoing process of progressive release suggested by Ken Poure in his book *Parents: Give Your Kid a Chance.*[1]

Here is a sample script starring John Jefferson, mythical teenager, with the opening scene taking place the day after his thirteenth birthday. Dad speaks first.

"John, be ready at six tonight. Your mother and I are taking you out to dinner."

John wasn't sure what was up, since he had never been invited out to dinner with his parents by himself. He appeared at six sharp, ready for whatever was to come. His dad drove by all the regular fast food restaurants, and before John knew it, he was eating a fabulous steak dinner.

When the meal was over, John's mom pulled out a wrapped package. What was going on? His birthday was yesterday! As he unwrapped the gift, he discovered a carved wooden box. Inside the box were several small cards. This really was a strange evening!

His dad began to explain, "John, your mother and I are excited about your growing up. In five short years you will be eighteen and will probably be leaving for college. We want you to be prepared to make your own decisions and run your own life.

"So, in the next five years, your mom and I want to help you on that road to independence by helping you establish some new freedoms and responsibilities each year. To help us do this, we will be giving you a box similar to this on each of your next four birthdays. Inside each box will be the freedoms and responsibilities we think you can handle in the next twelve months. We want you to look at them, and then we will discuss them together."

John pulled out several small cards from his wooden box and read:

1. Curfew
    Can stay out until 10:00 P.M. with these conditions:
    a. It is not a school night.
    b. We know and approve of where you are going and who you are with.
    c. The limit is one night per weekend.
    (Family functions and baby-sitting are exceptions. Curfew may be extended for school functions that go later than 10:00 P.M. Check with us beforehand.)

2. Phone Privileges
    You can have your own extension phone in your room. Just remember there are others in the family and leave us some talking time too!

3. Parties
    You can plan a big party and invite your friends, but we must be home.

4. Room
    You are responsible for the condition of your room: bed made, carpet vacuumed regularly, furniture dusted, clothes put away.

5. Clothes
    Mom will teach you how to use the washer and dryer and how to iron. You will find a new clothes hamper for your dirty clothes in your room.

6. Money

You can now manage your own money: budget money for school supplies, lunch, etc. An allowance will be given to you on a weekly basis.

Basically, John was pleased with his privileges and would accept his responsibilities. However, he thought he should be able to stay out until ten on both Friday and Saturday nights. Mom and Dad agreed to allow him to do so as long as he's up for church on Sunday.

Dad assured John, "We're not talking about perfection, but we do expect for you to do your best. If you manage your box well this year, then you'll move on to more privileges and responsibilities next year.

"Our goal is that you will be able to function pretty much as an adult by the time you leave home. Your mom and I have written up a possible plan of progression." Dad took out the rocket diagram (see illustration 5). "Let's look at it together and see if you think our plan is fair."

Again John and his parents discussed the goals they had set for him. Dad noted the progression from the first stage of the rocket (the box he just received) to the launched rocket, which signifies independence, at age eighteen.

John had a few suggestions. He felt that group dating should be allowed at age fourteen rather than fifteen. Dad and Mom discussed this with him, and they all agreed to this change.

"You can speed up these privileges, or slow them down," Dad assured John. "It's up to you and how you manage your box. We don't think you're going to disappoint us. We're looking forward to watching you become a responsible adult.

"Now, John, do you have any other questions?"

"Yeah, Dad," John said with a look of satisfaction on his face. "Could I have a banana split for dessert?"

Perhaps you, too, have questions. You see the benefits

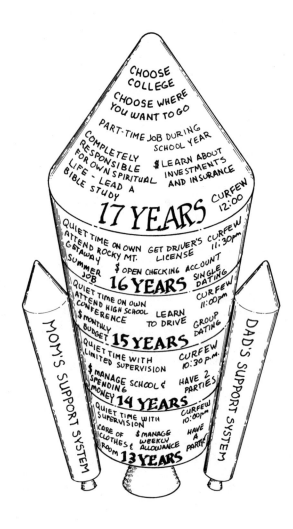

Illustration 5

of the Birthday Boxes, but you don't know how to adapt them to your unique situation.

First, you need an overall plan. You need to approach this in the same way you developed your adolescent's Teenage Challenge. Here are some areas to consider:

1. Curfew

We began at age thirteen with a curfew of 10:00 P.M., one night per weekend, and the stipulation that we approve of where the teen was going and who he was going with. At each birthday, we added thirty minutes to the curfew time so that at age seventeen, the curfew was midnight. At age eighteen, the teen set his own curfew.

Some mothers have commented to me that their thirteen-year-olds really didn't need a curfew as they were seldom out at night. Even so, it is helpful to establish the principle of the curfew before it is needed. Then each year you extend the curfew. Your sixteen year old, whose curfew may be 11:30, does not feel restricted, even though friends can stay out longer, because the curfew is thirty minutes later than when he or she was fifteen.

Our curfew is not an ironclad rule. We do make exceptions for special events and school functions. Also when a teen calls home to let us know he is running late, we are always willing to add a few minutes. We have avoided most of those late night adventures, but not all!

2. Academics, Homework

We began at age thirteen with limited supervision of homework and gradually worked toward their being totally responsible for their school work. This was not the same age for each of our teens, because it depended upon their maturity.

By the time our older boys were second semester seniors, homework was their business, even if they got their priorities mixed up, and sometimes they did. They learned a valuable lesson in managing their time, however, which benefited them as freshmen in college. Since they had already experienced "being on their own academically," they were able to handle the freedom of college life with much more responsibility.

3. Rooms

Once you put keeping their room clean in the Birthday Box, remember it is their responsibility. An occasional gift of mom's helping hand will be appreciated, but sometimes it is better to close the door than to infringe on this agreement. Remember this is a learning process.

In this area we have had very mixed results. One of our guys scored above average on housekeeping from the very beginning. Another lived in an unbelievable mess and got this responsibility in his Birthday Box for several years straight. Both finally got the picture: It's your responsibility, not ours. At least our boys know how to do basic housekeeping jobs by the time they leave home.

4. Grooming

At what age do you feel comfortable letting your son or daughter choose his or her own hair style? When can your teen handle the responsibility for shopping and selecting his or her own clothes?

Our boys have come home with the wrong sizes. One protested, "But the sales clerk told me this knit shirt would get bigger when it was washed."

"That's not usual," I replied, and then waited until the shirt was washed. The next time he bought a larger shirt.

When is your teen able to wash and iron his or her own clothes?

I have seen sweaters come out of the washing machine so small they looked like doll clothes, even though I cautioned the boys, "Look at the label before you wash it. If the sweater has to be cleaned, give it to me and I'll take it to the cleaners."

I've also noticed pink underwear, but these mistakes are part of the process. Too often grown men bring their dirty clothes home for mom to wash, but not our boys. When they visit us, their dirty clothes stay in their own clothes hampers.

5. Money

Some teens have a built-in knack for managing money and others have the knack for spending it! We started by letting our teens manage their money for school supplies and lunches. Once they showed signs of maturing, we added shopping for clothes and progressed from weekly allowances to monthly allowances.

We also included part-time and summer jobs in this area. At thirteen Joel mowed yards during the summer. At fourteen both Joel and Jarrett worked as counselors at a Boy Scout camp. It is difficult for a teen to get a steady job until he or she is sixteen.

Again, the standards we set varied for each individual boy. With all his extracurricular activities, Jarrett couldn't have worked and still accomplished his school work. Working, however, has kept Joel busy and out of trouble, since he is not a joiner. Obviously the teen's responsibilities at home will be less if he or she is working.

Once a teen begins to work and has a social security number, he or she should also open a checking account. You may want to require that a certain percentage of the money they earn be saved for college or a special purchase. It's wise to set this standard as a part of the Birthday Box.

6. Dating and Parties

To offset disappointment at not being able to date at thirteen, we put a tentative plan in their Birthday Box for when they could group date and single date. Seeing that these privileges were just around the corner kept them from rebelling.

At the same time we opened our home to their friends.

When Jarrett was in eighth grade, one of his privileges was to invite his friends over to our house every other Friday afternoon. Other moms were so appreciative they began to pitch in and help with these informal parties.

7. Spiritual Life

One important thing we did in the early teen years was to help our boys find devotional material on their level. Check out your local Christian bookstore for devotional books like *If God Loves Me, Why Can't I Get My Locker Open?* by Lorraine Peterson (Bethany House Publishers) and books on Christian beliefs and values like *How to Be Your Own Selfish Pig* by Susan Schaeffer Macaulay. A series of books that especially appeals to teens is the Campus Life series (published by Zondervan), which includes books like *The Trouble with Parents: How to Make Peace with Yours, Do You Sometimes Feel Like a Nobody?* and *A Love Story.* Reading at least one of these books a year was part of each Birthday Box. We also purchased an annual subscription to *Campus Life* magazine for our boys. The pages of this magazine were always dog-eared from use. (To subscribe to Campus Life, write: Campus Life Subscription Services, P.O. Box 1947, Marion, Ohio 43306).

We often included the privilege of attending a high school Christian conference in our boys' boxes. One summer Joel attended a Youth Congress for 25,000 high school students in Washington, D.C., and one winter he went on a Christmas ski retreat with our youth group.

Some families change churches during the teen years to find a good youth group for their adolescents. One mom included the privilege of choosing a church in the box for her daughter's fifteenth birthday because the daughter was very unhappy at the family's church. That year the daughter became very active in a church that had an excellent youth group.

Again, developing a plan when the teen is young and

still receptive to parental input insures a gradual transition from mom's and dad's beliefs to a teen's own values.

8. Driving, Meal Preparation, Sewing

Driving is a big privilege for a teen and often requires a full-fledged agreement within the Birthday Box structure. One mom in a support group and her son drew up the following contract together:

DRIVING CONTRACT

Seat Belts

1. I must wear a seat belt when I drive and so must anyone sitting in the passenger side of the front seat. In many states this is now state law.

2. Passengers in the backseat have the option to wear a seat belt.

Passengers

1. No more than two people in the front seat (including me).

2. No more than three people in the back.

Driving Range

In Knoxville, I can drive as far as the Shangri-la Farms, unless accompanied by an adult.

Curfew

Time is 10:00 P.M. If later, call before curfew and get permission to stay later.

Maintaining Grades

Grades must stay above a C average.

Punishments

1. If not in by curfew and have not called, one demerit. If I get four demerits, the car is taken away for a weekend.

2. If grades are below a C average, the car is taken away for all social events until grades improve.

3. Any speeding or parking tickets I get, I pay for myself.

Miscellaneous
1. Always tell parents where I'm going to be. If they aren't home, write a note and call later.
2. No one else shall drive my car because of insurance coverage.
3. No one under the influence of alcohol in the car.

Such a contract sets the driving rules from the very beginning. I know one mom whose teenage daughter was very cooperative and mature; but when her boyfriend, who was a year younger, pleaded to drive the family car, she allowed him to do so. He drove too fast in a twenty mile-per-hour zone, and the two teens were stopped by the police, who informed them that "A teen with a permit cannot drive a car unless the licensed driver has been driving over a year."

It had never occurred to the mother that her daughter would allow anyone else to drive the family car. She wishes she'd thought of a driving contract when her daughter was learning to drive; then there would have been no question about the family's rules of the road.

You may also want to include other areas in your teen's Birthday Box, such as meal preparation, sewing, and simple car mechanics. When one of our boys was a junior in high school, we included reading a book about investments and making an imaginary investment in the stock market. Whatever area you choose to include, the goal is the same: to develop the teen's competence to function productively in the adult world.

Parents should agree on a tentative plan first, using exercise 9 as a guide. You may want to include your teen in this part of the planning, or you may want to present the rocket as a surprise. Then prepare the rocket diagram (illustration 5). At the launching dinner, the teen makes suggestions, and a final plan is set, again using a rocket diagram.

Making the Box Special

Each year we take the teen out for a special dinner by himself. I also watch all year long for unique boxes. One year Jarrett's box was a wooden bank, another year, a wooden chess set.

Our boys display these boxes in their rooms and use them to store their personal items. By the time they are seventeen, they have five unique boxes, each a visible reminder of their growth toward independence.

Monitoring the Box

We have found it helpful to have a six-month or quarterly evaluation with our teen to discuss how he is doing. If the teen has a problem with self-discipline, we get together more often.

One of our boys kept asking, "How am I doing?" Since he was doing very well, we hadn't mentioned the box. After his comment, I realized he needed some positive feedback, so I began commenting occasionally, "You're really keeping up with your homework. I'd give you an A in that area."

What if your teen doesn't carry through with the responsibilities or abuses the privileges? If all else fails, give him or her the same box next year. If he or she fails in one area, just repeat that area. Remember your teen wants new freedoms. Once he understands they are accompanied by responsibilities, hopefully, he will not let you down.

One of our teens did not achieve in school, even though he was not lacking in intelligence. We made achieving a B average a part of his driving contract.

"Gee, Mom, I grew up in Austria. You can't drive there until you're eighteen so it's no big deal," he replied.

When his friends began to get their licenses, his attitude changed. Suddenly his grades began to improve.

With Joel, we found we needed to be flexible. Once we saw improvement in his grades and his attitude toward his studies, we allowed him to get his license, even though he did not have a B average. But he could only drive to work and to Christian activities. A year later he finally achieved a B average, and we received the good student discount on our insurance.

Before you tie grades into privileges, ask yourself, "What is reasonable for my teen?" Some kids work harder to maintain a steady C average than others do to make straight As.

Our teens knew that their progress toward new freedoms depended upon four factors: overall attitude, spiritual growth, attitude toward school, and how well they managed the box.

Some privileges can be speeded up by excelling in an area. For instance, Joel, who is a good manager of finances, had a checking account at fifteen instead of sixteen.

Alternative Approaches

You may want to begin the Birthday Box at eleven or twelve and omit the Teen Challenge. Perhaps your teen will enjoy the box at thirteen, but not again at fourteen, or will not cooperate if the Birthday Box is begun at fourteen or fifteen. Mothers in some support groups have adapted the boxes to high school and called them freshmen privileges, sophomore privileges, junior privileges, and senior privileges.

One mom learned about the Teenage Challenge and Birthday Box right before her son's fourteenth birthday, so she combined the two. The important thing is to set up a well-defined, progressive structure for increasing responsibilities and privileges each year.

BRIAN'S STEPS TO ADULTHOOD

1. You may choose your clothes and hairstyle.
2. Your homework will no longer be supervised, but we will be glad to help if asked.
3. Your bedtime is extended until 10:00 P.M. on school nights.
4. You will receive $60.00 allowance a month for spending money and school obligations. Extra money may be earned by doing yard or housework.

5. Your room is now your responsibility. Mom has the right to refuse to allow friends to visit if your room isn't clean.

6. You are responsible for the care of your clothes. Mom will teach you how to use the washer and dryer.

I know you can do it. I love you.

Mom

The teenage boy hung the document on his bedroom wall and is working to achieve these responsibilities. But my friend's story doesn't end there. When her sixteen-year-old son celebrated his birthday, she took him out to dinner and discussed his new responsibilities and privileges. He is now taking care of his clothes and among other things, learning how to use the microwave oven.

Her nine-year-old daughter watched this process and decided to get a headstart. That summer she listed her own goals, one of which was to place in an event in the city swim meet. She not only placed in several events, but also received the "Most Valuable Swimmer Award" for her local swim team.

"Megan was the only swimmer in our club that made and met her personal goals," her coach told her mother at the awards dinner.

STEPS TO DECISION-MAKING

Throughout this book I have been talking about helping your adolescent make his or her own decisions. Now I'd like to suggest four steps that expedite decision-making in your teen.

Allow Your Teen to Participate in Family Decisions.

Several years ago we had a major decision to make. Our job in Austria was drawing to a close, and we had decided to return to the United States. Jarrett was nearing college age, and the move to an American school system seemed timely. We had two possible locations, Atlanta or Knoxville.

We decided to bring our boys into this decision-making process. We sat down with each of the boys individually and talked through the pros and cons of each location, making a list as we went. Each boy saw more pros to moving to Knoxville, which was our old hometown.

At the end of each of these conversations, we said, "We really appreciate your input and will consider it seriously when we have to make the final decision. If God leads us to another location, how would you feel about it? Would you still be on our team?"

All three responded affirmatively, and our final decision matched the boys wish as we moved to Knoxville. Although many factors entered into making this decision, the boys felt good about being included in the discussion. The more family decisions teens can participate in, the more confident they become in their own decision-making ability.

Allow Your Teen to Choose between Options

Decision-making is easier for preteens and teens if they are given a choice between two or more options. Jonathan loved both basketball and skiing, but we knew he couldn't participate in both sports since the seasons overlapped.

"The decision's up to you, Jonathan," we said. "Since both basketball and ski racing have the same season, you must decide which one you want to do this year. You might want to list all the pros and cons of each sport, and then pick the one that seems best."

Jonathan decided on ski racing.

Once a decision has been made, we insist that the boys complete the commitment. For instance, when Jonathan signed up for the AYSO soccer league one fall, he was not allowed to quit until the season was over even though he wanted to. If he wanted to skip the league's spring season, that was all right, but he had to complete the commitment he had made for the fall season.

Part of decision-making is encouraging your adolescent

to develop his or her own thinking process. Try answering a question with a question. "Well, what do you think about that?" or "What do you think is the smart thing to do in this situation?" It's easy for me to give instant answers, so I have to check myself before I offer advice.

Allow Your Teen to Negotiate

Sometimes a teen has no trouble making a decision, but you can't go along with it.

When Joel was a senior in high school he was co-captain of the soccer team with practice every day for several hours after school. He was also working at the local tennis club on the weekends and wanted to add a work night during the week, which would include cleaning up the club after closing and getting home at midnight.

Dave and I had our doubts about this. "Let's sit down," I suggested, "and look at this situation logically. Get some paper, and let's list the pros and cons."

"Not the pros and cons again!" Joel moaned.

"You talk and I'll write. Now give me all the pros of why you should work on week nights." I waited patiently.

"Well," Joel said slowly, "there's money and money and money."

The pro list completed, I added several cons, such as loss of sleep and effect on studies.

At an impasse, Dave and I switched into the negotiation mode, going through three steps.

1. We stated the problem clearly: Joel wanted to work at night during the school week, and we didn't want him to.

2. We listed some possible options:
   a. Work only on weekends
   b. Work weekends and one school night
   c. Work weekends and afternoons
   d. Work weekends, two mornings before school, and vacuum the courts sometime during the week (This might involve some night work, but not as late as a complete cleanup.)

3. Choosing a plan of action was the last step we took, and we settled on the last option subject to the boss's approval, which was given.

Doesn't this take a lot of time? Yes. But we're in the process of helping our guys to become competent decision-makers. It would be simpler just to say, "Do this" or "Do that," but when would they learn to make their own decisions?

A book, which has helped our guys develop decision-making skills is *Go for It!* by Judy Zerafa (Workman Publishing).

Allow Your Teen to Make Wrong Decisions

The hardest part of teaching teens to make decisions is watching them make mistakes. I'll never forget the time Jarrett took his new Walkman on a ski team trip.

"Nothing will happen to my Walkman if I take it with me," he argued. "It will be so boring without music."

"I still don't think it's wise, but the decision is yours to make," I replied. I had not been in favor of his spending about eighty dollars for it in the first place. That, too, had been his decision.

Before he turned to go out of the room, I added, "But Dad and I want you to do one thing before making the final decision. Take a piece of paper and on one side list all the pros, the reasons you want to take the Walkman. Then on the other side, list all the cons, the reasons you shouldn't take the Walkman. After that, the decision is yours."

We expected him to make the right decision once he had weighed the cons against the pros. His paper looked something like this, and from his perspective the decision was obvious.

Pros
1. I want to take it.
2. I'll have music on the bus and won't get bored.
3. If the weather is bad and we can't ski one day, I'll have music.

4. I'll be able to choose what music I want to hear and won't have to listen to trash.
5. It's not heavy and won't be hard to pack.

Cons
1. Can't really think of any, except that there's a slight possibility the Walkman might get lost or stolen.

"I'm not sure the first item on your pro list, *wanting* to take the Walkman, is legitimate," I mentioned. "It's your wish, not an objective reason."

Jarrett didn't answer, so I asked one more question. "Are you sure you've considered all the cons? What about the possibility that the Walkman might get wet or be ruined in other ways?"

"That just adds one more con," Jarrett insisted, "so the pros win. I'm going to take my Walkman."

The next day as the bus pulled away from the school, we could see Jarrett's face, surrounded by the wire headset, in the window.

Oh how I wanted to say, "I told you so," when Jarrett arrived home from the trip *minus* one Walkman!

"I hid it under my pillow, Mom. I just didn't leave it lying around. Can you believe someone would actually steal it?" he lamented.

Refraining from answering that question, I said, "Jarrett, I'm really sorry it was stolen. I know how hard you worked to save money to buy it."

Jarrett could not afford to replace the Walkman, but he learned from this experience, and recently we watched him work through the same process in another, more important situation. If we start with the minors and let teens develop confidence and competence at that level, then we can move on to the majors. Losing a Walkman was tough on Jarrett, but it wasn't a major decision like buying a computer or choosing a college, during which he used the same decision-making process much more objectively.

Why Not Take a Chance?

Wise parents begin working toward their offspring's independence almost from the moment the child is born. Just as you hand the baby a spoon for eating, knowing he or she will probably plaster the wall with food, so you take chances all along the path. Much frustration for both the teen and parent can be eliminated by releasing areas of responsibility and freedom once the child becomes thirteen. Why not take the chance?

EXERCISE 9

Birthday Boxes

I. List all the things your teen needs to know before he or she leaves home.

II. By each area put when you think your teen will be ready to assume the responsibility.

III. Sketch two rocket ships, using illustration 5 as a guide. Insert the different areas and potential progression on each copy and give one to your teen.

IV. Answer the following questions:
   A. Am I releasing too much or not enough freedom to my teen?

   B. Am I giving my teen too much or not enough responsibility?

Chapter Eleven

MIDCOURSE CORRECTION

Dave and I had been out of town for several days to conduct a Marriage Alive seminar. While we were gone, the boys had stayed with good friends, but they had come home a few hours before we returned. As we walked into our home, I immediately smelled cigarette smoke. I walked over and kissed Jarrett hello. As I expected, his breath smelled of smoke.

Without taking time to gather either my thoughts or the facts, I immediately accused him, "Jarrett, you've been smoking! How could you? You've broken our trust."

"No, Mom," he responded to my attack, "I promise I haven't been smoking."

"Then what is that smell?"

"Some guys were smoking on the bus on the basketball trip last weekend. I am wearing the same clothes, and they must still smell of smoke."

This did not satisfy me or his dad. After all, how did the smoke from his clothes get into his mouth?

Upstairs Jarrett's room smelled of smoke. There were no signs of cigarettes, but the window was open a crack, and when I looked on the ground outside, I saw the cigarette butt.

Dave and I mentally reconstructed the crime. Jarrett had lit up in his room, heard us drive in the driveway, threw the cigarette out the window, and then raced into the kitchen. He had forgotten about the smell of smoke and Mom's excellent nose. This was not the first time we had talked to him about smoking or lying.

If you've ever tried to release teens, you know it's not without some disappointments and failures like this one. Maybe the problem is you've veered off course and are headed in the wrong direction. Midcourse correction is needed. Most of us can identify with one mom who wrote the following letter to God in a moment of sheer frustration:

Dear Lord,

I feel like such a failure. Our family seems to be crumbling apart. I want to turn in my Mother Button. Being a mother used to be fun, now it's just one big hassle! I only seem to be able to see the inadequacies in me, my husband, and the children. I'm tired of making decisions (which are usually wrong), of not being shown respect, of being ignored, of not being appreciated. Tonight I wish I had chosen anything but motherhood as my vocation.

I tell my daughter, "I love you," and she casually answers, "That's nice." I see my son tell his dad he doesn't want to play tennis with him, following his sister's wonderful example.

I feel I've tried so hard as a mother and that "nothing took." Failure is such a terrible feeling.

Please help me, God, to get out of my emotions and see life through your eyes.

A Weary Mom

Maybe you aren't to this point of desperation yet, but we all need some midcourse correction from time to time. Let's consider three different situations where it is indicated.

1. You, like the mom in the letter, have really tried but it just isn't working. Included in this category is the mom who has tried "too hard" and has pushed her teen farther from a close relationship.

2. Mom is a "late bloomer," with a history of bad communication. "It's too late to start trying to build a relationship that appears to be nonexistent," you say. "If only I had worked harder in the elementary years but somehow the years one to twelve just slipped by."

3. Mom has finally surrendered and given up on herself and on her teen, too!

The teen senses Mom is disappointed, and they are both surrounded by a fog of hopelessness. "What's the use of trying?" Mom says. "The relationship is already blown."

Do you identify with one of these three situations? If you're the mother of a preteen, you may not have reached this state yet. I suggest that you read this chapter so you can make a midcourse correction when you begin to sense some problems. If you're the mother of a teen, you may be basically on course and only need some fine tuning. Or maybe some major adjustments are needed to stay headed in the right direction.

Good News Ahead

Wherever you are, there is hope for midcourse correction. But it doesn't start with your preteen or teen, it starts with you. We can't change other people but we can change ourselves. Then others sometimes change their responses to the person we have become.

The one element that has given me the power to change and apply the principles shared in these pages is my relationship with Jesus Christ. Without Him, *Almost Thirteen* is just another self-help effort without the gas to fuel the good intentions. I believe it's time to get back to the basics, back to the One who created parent-teen relationships in the first place. He wants to have a personal relationship with each of us through His son, Jesus Christ. And not only does He want to give us the power to implement His principles in our parent-teen relationships, but He also wants to give us purpose and meaning in our lives.

What's Real Security?

We each need to have a sense of security along with a good self-image, and in chapter 4, I encouraged us to build up our preteens. Our need for security demands that we be loved unconditionally.

Have you ever tried to love your preteen unconditionally? You get an extra point for trying, but only God can offer us that kind of love. His love was so unconditional that He was willing to give His only Son for a world that had rejected Him. Consider John 3:16, a verse you probably memorized in Sunday school. Stop for a minute and put your name in the blank: "For God so loved _____ that He gave His only begotten Son, that whoever believes in Him should not perish but have eternal life."

Nothing we will ever do will cause God to stop loving us. The apostle Paul tells us this in Romans 8:38-39. Imagine that he is speaking directly to you. "For I am persuaded," Paul says, "that neither death nor life, nor angels nor principalities nor things present nor things to come, nor powers, nor height nor depth, nor any other created thing, shall be able to separate _____ from the love of God which is in Christ Jesus our Lord."

This is real security! Even John Lennon, in one of his most popular Beatles' songs, wrote, "All we need is love!" If people are so aware of this need for love, why aren't all of us experiencing God's unconditional love in our lives? Let me suggest two possible reasons.

Perhaps you never fully understood why Christ came. Now that you've read John 3:16 as if God were speaking to you, you know Christ died to save you from your sins and give you eternal life.

Secondly, perhaps you have chosen to go your own way, like the defiant teenager who said, "No thanks, God, I'd rather do it myself!"

If you're in the first category, as I once was, you just need more information. If you're in the second category, it is time to consider the facts once again. Maybe you've rejected a caricature of what you think Christianity is without really considering Christ.

Let me share an experience in our home, which will help illustrate true Christian doctrine.

Broken Horses

One of our favorite souvenirs of our years in Europe is a ceramic horse, which sits on our coffee table. When we bought him as a second at a ceramic factory, we knew he had a patched-up broken leg, but we didn't care. That white Austrian Lippizan horse, made famous by the Spanish Riding School in Vienna, was a souvenir of our years in Austria.

Living with three active boys and all their friends is a precarious existence for a ceramic horse. Several times I screamed, "Watch out!" to the boys as they ran too close to the table. One day the inevitable happened. As we gathered up the pieces, putting it together again looked like an impossible job. We realized we had several alternatives.

1. We could say, "Accidents happen. It's broken too badly to ever repair. Let's throw it into the trash."

2. We could try to glue all the pieces back together again, a solution that might have worked until the horse was put under a little stress.

3. We could take our broken horse to a potter who makes ceramic horses and let him put it together again, although this would be very costly.

After discussion, we decided to take the horse to the expert, and now it's prettier than before. The specialist remolded the broken parts and refired the horse so it is even impossible to see where the leg was broken.

Repaired Lives; Repaired Relationships

Our horse is also special to us because it is a picture of what God has done for each member of our family and is willing to do for anyone who asks.

Look around you today. You will see lives broken into as many pieces as our horse was. You will see relationships between parents and children just as broken.

Paul says, "For all have sinned and fall short of the glory of God"(Rom. 3:23). Perhaps you are like I was, and the word *sin* doesn't really relate very well to you. So I ask you,

"Are you worried? Irritable? Self-centered?" These are the symptoms of sin.

Basically, sin is going our own way, completely indifferent to God. Our rebellion, like our preteens', may be noticeable to other people; or it can be a passive indifference.

We may have already committed our lives to Christ, but we have not extended this commitment to our relationship with our preteen or teen. We may have shut this area of our life off from the Lord's healing power because we are afraid of how He might ask us to change. Perhaps we are too strict and unloving or we selfishly ask too much of the child. Maybe the child is into drinking or drugs and is very difficult to love, or the adolescent is a stepchild with the maternal bond between mother and child lacking. If it seems impossible to love him or her, we certainly don't want God to remind us to "Love one another as I have loved you."

As with our horse, there are three options open to us.

1. We can say, "My life is all broken and messed up. There's really nothing that can be done. I won't even try!" Many people today just give up, because they don't realize there are other options. They don't listen to God's whisper in their lives or they don't hear him say, "I will help you love _____. Just trust me."

2. Some people try a do-it-yourself repair program. Self-reform may appear to be working for a while, but it shatters again when the stresses and strains of life inevitably come along.

3. We can place the broken pieces of our lives into the hands of the Master who created us.

God has the power to put us together again. This is very costly and, unlike our horse, we can never pay for it. God has already paid dearly by sacrificing His only Son, Jesus Christ, in our place. Paul tells us, "...God demonstrates His own love toward us, in that while we were still sinners, Christ died for us."

If God has paid in advance, what is our part?

All we have to do is accept his gift of salvation. Christ

stands at the door of each of our lives, but the handle is on the inside. "Behold, I stand at the door and knock," He says. "If anyone hears My voice and opens the door, I will come in to him..." (Rev. 3:20).

What do you answer? Again the choice is yours. You can say, "Go away!" You can ignore the knock, or you can open your life to Christ and invite Him in.

If you do, you might wish to pray this prayer. "Lord Jesus, I need You. I open the door of my heart and receive You as my Savior and Lord. Thank You for dying for me and for forgiving my sins. Take control of my life and turn my relationship with _____ into what You desire it to be. Thank You for coming into my life as You promised You would if I asked in faith."

Maybe you have already made such a commitment. "I know I'm a Christian," you say, "but I still feel defeated in my relationship with my child."

Achieving a personal relationship with God is the first step in overcoming defeat, but it doesn't guarantee a totally Christian relationship. Stop now and evaluate how you are relating to your child. Do you treat him or her with the same respect and courtesy that you give a good friend? Are you applying the love described in First Corinthians 13? Or do you have your child on a performance basis? That's not how God relates to you.

Janice was caught in this trap. Both she and her husband were Phi Beta Kappas in college. They had never thought that their son would be only an average student. In elementary school, Janice worked with the boy to help him achieve good grades, but in junior high he began to resent his mom's help. Slowly his grades dropped to Bs and Cs. Janice's own self-esteem was hurt by her son's poor performance and his seeming rejection of her help.

Their relationship continued to go downhill. Finally her son decided, *I just can't please my parents, so why try?* His B and C grades became Ds and Fs. Was Janice a Christian? Yes. Did she want to be a good mother? Yes. But she had forgotten that her self-worth comes from being a child of God, not from her children and their achievements. She also needed to realize it's all right to be average. As one person said, "God must have a special place in his heart for average people; He made so many of them!"

If you are not living out your Christian commitment in your relationship with your child, you may want to say this prayer as a renewal of your commitment to Him and to put your relationship with your preteen or teen into His hands. "I will love _____, Lord Jesus, with your help."

Now What?

We would all like to see a dramatic improvement in our relationship with our child, but more likely the change will be gradual. Remember, Christianity is not a feeling; it is a commitment that we renew each day when we determine to allow God to run our lives.

None of us needs to look to our child for affirmation. We must find our security and significance in our relationship with the Lord. We are of ultimate worth as His children. The result? We are free to love our teens with God's unconditional love; and if it's unconditional, it's not dependent on any human response or behavior.

Now that we have the power for mid-course correction, let's consider two areas that may need some work:
1. Rebuilding trust
2. Learning to deal with a resistant teen

REBUILDING TRUST

One day I decided to try to see myself as my boys saw me. I asked each of them separately, "If you could change one thing about me, what would it be?"

One son answered, "You would totally trust me!"

Fritz Ridenour, in his book *What Teenagers Wish Their Parents Knew about Kids*, says he tells his parenting classes and seminars one basic thing: "You might as well trust your teenager; you don't have any other reasonable choice. Distrust simply breeds more distrust, but if you keep trusting your teenager, sooner or later the message will get through."[1]

Five Trust-busters

If you and your preteen do not have a trusting relationship, now is the time to begin to build trust. Start by deciding where the two of you lost the natural trust that exists between parent and child. Consider these five possible trust-busters.

Trust-buster 1—A single mistake:
Adolescents often do something wrong and the parent responds, "If I can't trust you in this area, how can I trust you in other areas?"

Trust is not a one-time gift, however; trust must be freely given time and time again. After Jarrett wrecked my parents' car, my feeling was, *How can we ever trust our son again? He deceived us. He may do it again.*

At the same time Dave and I realized that unless we were willing to reinvest some trust, Jarrett had no way to rebuild that trust. Our decision? We told Jarrett, "This has been a real learning situation, and we feel you're learning the importance of being open and honest with us. That's real progress. Let's continue to work together on this, and I believe we can rebuild the trust between us in twenty-four hours."

Our relationship was restored, and we moved on from there.

Trust-buster 2—Judging guilty without a fair trial:
Everyone deserves a fair hearing. Do you see your preteen or teen as innocent until he or she is proven guilty? Unfortunately parents sometimes assume the worst before all the facts are known.

One fall, when Dave and I took Jarrett back to college, we allowed Joel and Jonathan to stay by themselves. One of our requests was that they attend Sunday school and church.

When we returned home, Joel's khaki slacks were not precariously perched on a chair in his room as they always were when he had changed into sports clothes after church. I was about to convict him without a trial when I casually asked him, "Did you really go to Sunday school and church?"

"Yeah, we went, but we were late to Sunday school. I changed clothes in the laundry room when we got back," Joel replied.

Sure enough, there were his clothes on the floor by the washing machine. I was glad I had kept quiet until I knew all the facts.

Trust-buster 3—Lack of freedom:

Sometimes parents tell their teen, "Earn our trust and then we'll trust you." Then they establish ironclad rules, which give the teen no leeway.

I ask these parents, "How can your child prove he or she is trustworthy without being given some freedom to make decisions?"

Soon after Joel got his license, we let him drive to work at the tennis club. One morning when Dave opened the trunk to get a bag of books he had left there, to his surprise the books were strewn all over the trunk. How could the books be jostled like that? Joel had been doing figure eights in the parking lot of the tennis club. He received a stern lecture about racing around parking lots at night, but we did not prohibit him from driving the car to work. Why? If we had said, "Earn our trust, and then we'll let you drive again," we would have eliminated his opportunity to be more careful in the future. Real parental trust cannot exist without some adolescent freedom.

Trust-buster 4—Reciting a litany of failures:

Parents tend to recall a teen's past mistakes and failures whenever the child talks back or argues with them. Sometimes they have really never forgiven the child for that earlier mistake. We need to erase our children's mistakes each night and start the next morning with a clean slate.

A teenage girl once told me, "My mother won't let me forget the one night I came in drunk. You'd think she'd realize it was a terrible experience for me. I'd never had anything to drink before, and I got sick and threw up in my date's car. I was horrified.

"I told Mom all about it, but now, whenever I go out, she tells me not to drink and reminds me of that night. Why can't she be quiet and give me another chance?"

I can understand this mother's fears for her daughter, but constantly reminding the girl of this failure will not build trust for the future. Why didn't Mom thank Ann for telling her the truth? Then they could have talked through the experience together, why it happened and what Ann might do if she were confronted again with the same temptation.

Trust-buster 5—Parental evasion of the problem:

Sometimes parents react to a preteen's lying or sneakiness by talking about trust rather than by discussing the individual incident and how to solve it. "How can I trust you when you are continually lying to me?" the parent asks.

Instead, the parent could say, "Look, we want to build our relationship, not tear it down. It would help tremendously if I could count on your being honest with me. Let's try this for the next twenty-four hours. I'll try not to attack you, and you try to stick to the truth."

After my outburst about Jarrett's smoking, I realized I had to calm down and get out of the attack mode. When Dave and I were ready to work through the situation with him, I purposely avoided the question of "Where did I go wrong?" and instead concentrated on "Where do we go from here?"

Jarrett still maintained he was innocent, even though his guilt was obvious.

"Jarrett, we do believe in miracles, but we see no reason why God would allow a cigarette to smoke itself in your bedroom and then hop out the window. I would also be dumb to ignore the obvious sign of smoke on your breath," I said.

At this point Dave picked up the ball. "As I see it, we are dealing with two issues here: first, smoking; second, lying. Frankly, Jarrett, your mother and I are much more concerned with the second issue. We all have weak areas and a tendency toward certain mistakes. We know you've been working hard in this area; don't let a relapse set you back."

After a little more persuasion, Jarrett admitted his mistake and was ready to accept the consequences, the loss of his privileges for a week. We were all ready to move on, but I felt I had to renew the trusting relationship that had existed between Jarrett and me, so the next day I wrote Jarrett this letter:

Dear Jarrett,

Today my thoughts keep coming back to the unbelievable welcome we gave each other yesterday. Wish we could do it over again. So you experimented again with cigarettes—big deal! Growing up I did the same.

I'm really not concerned that you'll become a smoker. You're analytical and intelligent, and you know cigarettes can be harmful to your health. I trust your judgment in this area. If you choose to smoke once you're eighteen, it's your decision.

What I wish I could change about last night was my initial reaction. I made it very difficult for you to be open and honest with me. That's the real issue. If I had waited until I was in control of my own feelings, perhaps you would have chosen honesty instead of deception. Let's work together on this area during the next few weeks.

My Part: I will try not to put you on the spot. If you

feel I'm attacking you, please say, "Wait, Mom, I feel at-
tacked. Let's start this conversation over again."

Your Part: You choose to be open and transparent
with me, to tell the truth even if it's incriminating.

Let's build back that trust quickly. I think even twenty-
four hours of openness could do it.

Love,

Mom

BEGINNING AGAIN

Obviously the first way to rebuild trust is to determine to
avoid these five trust-busters. Then we need to replace the
negative with the positive by giving the gift of trust to our
teens. This seemingly risky and costly investment has been
known to pay excellent dividends.

Dr. Norm Wright, director of Christian Marriage Enrichment, gives this advice: "Trusting your teen means running
the risk of having that trust broken. It might be nice if you
could get your adolescent to promise in writing not to betray
your trust; you could even get it notarized. But it would only
be a piece of paper. As in any love relationship, you have to
risk being hurt. You'll be disappointed, just as I've been at
times. That's the price of saying, 'I still love you.'"

What if a teen lies again and again or if drug abuse or
promiscuous sex is involved? Surely, you don't just put your
head in the sand and blindly trust. At this point you may
think your teen has given up his privacy rights by default,
and you as a parent must do what you can to supervise and
direct your misguided child.

If the situation is chronic, I suggest that you seek professional help from a counselor or psychiatrist, preferably
someone who shares the Christian perspective. In these
pages we are discussing ordinary situations where there's
time to reinvest and rebuild trust. As long as you have good

open communication, rebuilding trust should not be an impossible task.

Trust Yourself

We not only need to trust our teens, we need to trust ourselves. We do try to be good parents. I may not always be consistent with our boys, but over the years I have tried to be. I might have a specific plan, like the Teenage Challenge and Birthday Boxes. Sometimes they work. Other times I have to hope that my common sense will get me through the difficult times.

Trust God

We need to trust God. I have been able to keep going when my teens are causing trouble because I know God is totally committed to me and to my teens. How do I know this? Listen to God's promise in Psalm 138:8: "The Lord will perfect that which concerns me."

When I need hope for the future, I remember verses like: "But if we hope for what we do not see, then we eagerly wait for it with perseverance"(Rom.8:25) and "he who plows should plow in hope" (1 Cor. 9:10). *The New Strong's Exhaustive Concordance* lists all the Bible verses that contain the word *hope* in them. When I'm feeling blue, I read through some of these verses.

Pray

Motherhood is not a solitary occupation. We have a backup in the resources of the living God which we can call up through the medium of prayer.

For several years I have kept a prayer diary for each of our boys, and I have found this system really works for me. I keep my prayer log in my daybook with my "to do" lists. Each year Dave and I also make out a prayer list for the boys for the coming year. Some of the items on our list for Jonathan when he was almost thirteen were:

1. His relationship with God would be alive and growing.
   a. He would have confidence that the Lord's way is best.
   b. He would develop a regular quiet time.
   c. He would apply biblical knowledge to daily situations.
   d. He would see answers to his prayers.
2. He would have a high standard of conduct and develop the right convictions.
3. He would work toward academic success.
   a. He would develop a love for reading.
   b. He would give his studies his best effort.
   c. He would work toward good relationships with teachers and other students.
4. He would develop self-esteem.

After a page of my desires for each boy, I keep a running diary. Here I write down my prayers about daily events. I always try to state my prayers in a positive way. For instance, I write, "Please motivate Joel to do his best this week," rather than, "Please help Joel overcome his laziness."

When I give my concerns to God in prayer, I find I don't nag my teens as much. The problems are in God's hands so I don't have to worry so. When I see God answering my prayer, I write the date and the answer across from the request. I can look back over the years and see all God has done in our lives.

(See prayer journal forms in the daybook, *The Time Maker,* Thomas Nelson Publishers.)

DEALING WITH A RESISTANT TEEN

"It's not that my daughter is not pliable, she's completely brittle," one mom commented to me. "There's no flexibility at all. When we disagree, there's always resistance."

How can you deal with a resistant teen? If I possessed the answer to that question, I would be world famous. However, I can say that the younger the resistant adolescent, the easier it is to improve the relationship.

While strong-willed adolescents are more likely to be resistant, a strong will can be a positive characteristic. Look at the great leaders of our world, I often reminded myself when our oldest son came close to teenage rebellion.

I once told him, "I'm glad you didn't become a rebellious teen." Then I had to admit my curiosity, "What kept you from it?"

"I just decided not to," he answered bluntly.

Later, when I began writing this book, I asked him again. "You said you were tempted to be rebellious, but you chose not to be. What advice would you give to teens who feel rebellious?"

Jarrett thought for a while, then he answered, "Well, I would tell them, 'You might get what you want for a while, but in the end, no one will win.' It's as if you're standing on the edge of a cliff. Why don't you jump off? Because you know what the end results would be."

Jarrett weighed the benefits against the final consequences. When he put staying out all night or some other adventure on one side of the scale and his relationship with his parents on the other, the relationship had much greater weight to him.

Here are some tips from some mothers who learned to cope with their resistant teens:

Give the Teen as Much Freedom as Possible.

Tightening the noose only causes the resistant teen to struggle against you even more. Say Yes whenever possible.

Always ask yourself, "Is this a moral issue?" Make sure your No remains a No.

Your strong-willed teen will respect you much more if you are consistent. Discuss the issue, let your teen express feelings freely, and if you make a mistake, admit it. But do not be talked into a verdict reversal just to get the teen off your back.

The summer after Jarrett's freshman year in high school, he worked as a counselor at a Boy Scout camp in Germany. We were still living in Vienna, and had planned our family vacation so we could get Jarrett at camp ten days before school began.

One night Jarrett called us from the camp. He told us about an Air Force sergeant he had met. Then he said, "Sergeant Brooks has invited me to spend a whole week with him at Ramstein Air Force Base. Isn't that great? You won't have to pick me up. I can take a train back to Vienna.

"While he works, I can watch videos and visit the PX and buy Pop Tarts and Dr. Peppers," he exclaimed.

All the American goodies we can't buy in Austria, I thought.

Dave and I had learned not to give immediate answers to major questions, so Dave told him we would call him back. Many factors led to our final decision to say no: we didn't know this sergeant, we had planned our vacation around getting Jarrett to save a train ticket, and we felt he needed the ten days of rest before school started.

There were some heated discussions after we told him our decision, but in the end he was willing to go along with us. Did he think we made a mistake? Yes! Even now, years later, he sincerely believes we were wrong. (In reading this chapter, Jarrett asked that this statement be changed to: "Even now, years later, he knows they were wrong.") And we still believe we were right.

The real issue was not that we had to say no this time, but that Jarrett accepted our decision and authority. The words *authority* and *resistance* seem to be like oil and water. They just won't mix. But if we give as much as we can, the few big no's are more likely to be accepted. In effect Jarrett was saying, "I value our relationship more than getting what I want in this instance."

Again, let me add that this approach may work with young teens whose parents still have good leverage but not with older teens.

Respect your Teen's Privacy.

Merton Strommen says in his book *Five Cries of Parents,* "Respect for the privacy of adolescents, an important aspect of nurturance, indicates parents' belief in their children's right to have a life space of their own. More than that, it is an important ingredient in building trust. Parents who listen to phone conversations or open and read letters are violating the adolescent's desire not to reveal every aspect of himself or herself to others. Throwing out clothes, magazines, or records belonging to the adolescent, or going through desk and dresser drawers, are actions that often result in alienation instead of togetherness."[2]

Snooping will erode relationships and breed distrust. Trust God to reveal to you the problems you need to know.

Resist the Urge to Dote.

The more we can relate on an adult-to-adult level with our resistant teen, the better.

Older Teens Present Special Problems.

Here are some ideas from a mom whose son had a rocky history of drinking, failing grades, expulsion from school, and wrecked cars.

"Parents who lose control of younger teens have special problems in the later teen years. I have learned that I must give up my desire to manipulate and control my son. God gives His children the freedom of choice. We are to do the same.

"It's really hard, but I've tried to turn my son completely over to God. Since he refuses my advice, suggestions, and opinions, I try to give none. I have actually told him he is now in God's hands. When he asks me a question, I tell him to ask God. This places God's pressure on him, not me."

Once she learned these principles in a Moms' Support Group, this mother held firm to them. Now her son is in college and working part-time, his grades are good, and their relationship is healthy and growing.

Moms in my support groups have found three books especially helpful in living with the resistant teenager: *Parents in Pain* by John White (InterVarsity Press), *How to Really Love Your Teenager* by Ross Campbell (Victor Books), and *The Wounded Parent* by Guy Greenfield (Baker Books).

Summing Up

I think Fritz Ridenour sums up midcourse correction when he says, "After parenting three kids of my own, and talking to a lot of them I didn't parent, I am convinced that the relationship between parent and child is primary. Whatever happens between you and your teenager is commentary on the kinds of attitudes you are bringing to that relationship."[3]

A change in your relationship with your preteen or teen can start today. You can give your child the gift of trust, and you can deal with resistance in the ways these other moms suggest. Allow God to help you through this necessary process.

PART FIVE

Relax:
Accepting Things
You Cannot Change

Chapter Twelve

RELAX! WHO ME?

The week that Jarrett graduated from high school was unbelievably hectic. Still I surveyed our first graduate with pride, for he really was fast becoming an adult.

One evening during graduation week Jarrett's friend, Andy, was staying overnight, and at ten o'clock, Jarrett announced, "Mom, Andy and I need to run over to Andy's house to pick up something. I'll call you from there."

"Don't you dare," I replied. "I'm exhausted. I'm going to bed!"

I am a light sleeper and have never developed the ability to sleep soundly when an Arp teen is still on the loose so I woke up at 2:00 A.M. and discovered that Jarrett and Andy were still not home.

What do you do when you wake up and your teen is not home? Do you call the hospital? The police? Only a parent who has experienced it knows that helpless feeling when there is really nothing you can do. Although I felt that Jarrett was probably all right, I still had a gnawing feeling in the pit of my stomach as slowly the minutes turned into half an hour and finally an hour. At three o'clock I heard the car turn into the driveway. How did I feel? Relieved. Tired. Mad. Mostly, though, thankful that Jarrett and Andy were safe.

I even had to laugh when the boys walked into the kitchen in Army fatigues and blacked faces.

"Jarrett," I began, "I was afraid you and Andy had been in an accident. Do you know what time it is? Where have you been?"

"Gee, Mom," my smooth-talking son replied, "thanks for worrying about us."

Worrying is not my favorite activity, but I guess it's nice to be appreciated. Just where had these two dignified high school graduates been, dressed so ridiculously? Writing a toilet-paper greeting to a girlfriend in her backyard!

Are you awakening in the night, as I did, wondering where your teen is? Are you worrying about your teen's grades, latest fad, choice of music, friends, college selection? Are you fearful when you hear a siren? Anxiety tends to appear in moms who feel responsible for events that are often out of their control.

For years we spent our time and energies training our children. Now that they are teens they must begin to make their own decisions. There are still times for advising, but there are also times for letting go. It's hard to watch them squirm under the pressure of peers or too many commitments, to see them crushed by unthinking friends and carried away on a sea of emotions. Relax in the middle of all this? Who me? Are you crazy? How can we relax when we feel responsible for things we can't control?

FLYING THE BUMPS

Perhaps you are like me and are not always relaxed on airplane trips, especially the bumpy ones! One friend said, "I work so hard helping the pilot when I fly, I never relax. Besides it's hard for me to pray on my knees with my seatbelt fastened!"

Recently I was flying in bad weather and with each bump, I thought of a new threat. *Maybe we are getting into a hurricane. Maybe we'll hit a wind shear!*

Then the captain came on the loudspeaker and said, "For the next hour or two it will be a little bumpy, since we are flying just on top of the clouds. After about an hour, it should be a smooth flight." I began to relax now that I knew to expect a few bumps. How great to know I was traveling on top of them!

The teenage years are like that rough flight. Realizing we're on top of the bumps helps us to relax, and if moms can relax during these years, they can look forward to smooth flying in years to come. However, there are two personality types who seem to have trouble relaxing. Do you recognize yourself as one of these?

The Interference Runner Has Trouble Relaxing.

Do you ever feel you should be a blocker for the local high school football team because you spend so much time running interference between your teen and his dad? Margaret had worked at trying to release her daughter, Jill. She felt she was doing well, especially on this lovely Saturday morning. Jill and her younger brother had each spent the night at a friend's house, and Margaret was relaxing and enjoying a second cup of coffee with her husband when the phone rang. Jill was having a haircut by herself this morning, and her mother thought Jill was calling to be picked up.

"Oh, Mom, I'm ruined!" Jill sobbed. "He cut the top too short! And left the back too long! Dad will shoot me. My friends will laugh at me!"

"We'll see if it can be fixed," Margaret said to soothe her daughter. "I'll come for you immediately." As she hung up the phone, Margaret also wondered what Jill's dad would say. He didn't like anything extreme, especially odd hair styles, and Margaret knew that too short on top and too long in the back meant Jill's hairdo was punk.

When they entered the house, Margaret quickly joined Jill in the bathroom to attempt to repair the damage with water, a blow dryer, and a curling iron. Fortunately, dad's reaction was, "That's not so bad," but he still asked, "Why didn't you go with her to make sure the haircut was done correctly?"

Margaret knew he wasn't ready for an explanation of

the four Rs and the principle of releasing teens. She felt as if it was the fourth quarter and she was losing!

Some moms are afraid to tell their husbands when a teen has lied or gotten into trouble, because they are afraid the dads will become angry and blow their relationships with their teenagers. Others must run interference in other areas, between brothers and sisters or grandparents and grandchildren or teens and teachers, and this certainly interferes with relaxation.

The Life Shaper Has Trouble Relaxing

Often moms take each event too seriously. Many events and decisions are out of their control so they become frustrated. Others, in their desire to protect their children, sometimes give them too much help.

The year that Jarrett was applying to colleges, I succumbed to the life-shaping urge. Fortunately, a good friend reminded me that I was trying to give too much help, so I backed away and allowed Jarrett to be responsible for the deadlines. Although not *every* application was sent, no deadline was missed for the schools he was really interested in. It's hard to stand by when your teen procrastinates with a reading assignment or misses cheerleading practice. You could remind him about these things, but from past experience you know a friendly reminder can be counterproductive.

One of our teens made the following statement about my helpful reminders. "Mom, you don't have to tell me the obvious like, 'Isn't it wonderful that God provided a snow day so you can get caught up on your school work.' "

We need to remember that character is sometimes built through failure. It's best to allow our teens to make some mistakes while they are still living at home.

In her excellent book, *Help, I've Just Given Birth to a*

Teenager, Pat Baker, a typical mom, shares from her experience.

It was difficult for my husband and me to decide when complete freedom of choice should begin. We decided to gradually give our daughters an increasing freedom of choice through the teen years....By allowing them to make their own choices at this time, we were close enough to give them support and offer guidance. During this time I had to muster up all the faith I had ever reserved and activate the trust I said I had in our daughters.[1]

Can you identify with Pat Baker? Is it scary to think about all the mistakes teens can make if they are allowed to fail? How can you relax? Here are four ways other mothers have managed to relax during the teen years.

RELAXATION AID 1: Develop an interest outside the home.

Often your teen zaps your emotional energy, and you seem to have less time for yourself. It's good to get out of the house and develop some activities of your own. You might join a volunteer organization whose goals coincide with your own interests. For instance, if you like to help people who are sick, join the women's auxiliary of your local hospital. You might join or organize a Moms' Support Group.

I've also found that physical activity helps me overcome the emotional stress of raising teens. I can vent my anger and disappointment when I hit the tennis ball, so I look forward to my weekly tennis league. One of my friends twists away her frustrations in jazzercise class, others jog or swim. I encourage you to find some physical outlet.

RELAXATION AID 2: Build the relationship with your husband.

Men were husbands first, not just fathers of teens. Studies show that the hardest times in the sexual relationship is when children are small and again when they are teens.

One wife commented to me, "We seem to disagree more now about the children than ever before." Another mom added, "It seems our whole relationship is centered around our teenagers, discussing their problems and trying to come up with solutions or discussing our own hurt feelings. It's as if we're not people any more, just parents of teens. This must stop!"

What can you do to build your relationship with your husband? I suggest that you begin to date again. Take time each week to be alone and to grow together in your marriage. You may be wondering, *When would we ever find time with all our teen's activities?*

Why not have breakfast or lunch together each week? One couple we know has a standing date each Monday evening while their son is at Boy Scouts. You might begin by having the ten dates Dave and I outlined in our book, *Ten Dates for Mates*. Remember the precaution, discussing your teen is an absolute no-no on these dates.

Also, consider a weekend away alone with your mate to concentrate on your marriage and forget the children for a few short days. We try to do this several times a year. In a few short years, your teens will be gone, but life and your marriage will go on. Start building today for *your* future as well as your preteen's.

RELAXATION AID 3: Get enough sleep and rest.

Late nights are as much a part of caring for a teenager as they are caring for a baby. Weekends, which used to be reserved for family fun, are now work times for mom and dad. One wise mom in a support group told how each Monday morning after getting her teens off to school, she would crawl back in bed and sleep until noon.

Since this routine is not practical if you have a job outside of the home, perhaps you could keep Monday nights free so you can go to bed early. I try to plan a light schedule for Fridays in anticipation of a busy weekend, but it doesn't always work out that way.

Almost everyone needs to find some extra time both to get everything done and still have time to rest. Why not analyze how you are spending your time? I used the simple process, the Hensley Grid, which was developed by Dr. Dennis E. Hensley, author of *Staying Ahead of Time* (see illustration 6). I made seven copies of this chart and carried one around with me each day for seven days. Each day I wrote in what I did during the various thirty-minute time slots, for instance, from 3:00 to 4:00 P.M. on weekdays: Drove carpool.

You may be in for some real surprises. Did you really spend that many hours on the phone last week? Maybe you should have taken an afternoon nap instead!

RELAXATION AID 4: Develop a sense of humor.

If joking comes naturally in your home, you're fortunate. Some families are natural cutups while others have to try to keep the atmosphere light.

In our home we place cartoons and jokes on the refrigerator door. We also try to look for the humor in each situation, like the famous case of "The Twinkle-toes Scuffs."

I'm sure you know how discouraging it is to clean and wax the kitchen floor, and then, only a few hours later, find new black scuff marks. Finally, in desperation, I put a notice on the refrigerator door:

WANTED:
NOTORIOUS TWINKLE-TOES

$1.00 Reward

to anyone giving information leading to the identification of Twinkle-toes, the criminal who leaves black marks on the kitchen floor.

The response? Light laughter from our boys, but the black marks appeared less frequently.

To solve the problem of the school books, jackets, and soccer cleats that were cluttering the small hall between our back door and the kitchen, I created Mom's Moving Service. I began with a media campaign, notices on the refrigerator door:

SAFE ECONOMICAL MOVING SERVICE

Use
Mom's Moving Service
10 cents an item. We aim to please.

The boys got the point, and Jonathan even paid his moving bills.

Another time I sent Joel an invitation to a Room Cleaning Party. And there was the time I gave Jarrett a Grump Coupon!

GRUMP COUPON
Good for Two Hours as a Grump
To redeem, simply present coupon to Mom.

Look for the humor in each heavy or irritating situation. Once Joel and I made the same mistake. I left my garden shoes and he left his soccer cleats just outside the back door. The next morning one of each was missing. We still laugh and look for the neighborhood dog who wears one soccer cleat and one garden shoe. Remember, laughter and relaxing go together.

THE HENSLEY GRID

	Monday	Tuesday	Wednesday	Thursday	Friday	Saturday	Sunday
8:00 / 8:30							
9:00 / 9:30							
10:00 / 10:30							
11:00 / 11:30							
12:00 / 12:30							
1:00 / 1:30							
2:00 / 2:30							
3:00 / 3:30							
4:00 / 4:30							
5:00 / 5:30							

Illustration 6

Now take the time to work through exercise 10 to direct your relaxation campaign. Let me also suggest that you read the following chapter written by our fourteen-year-old Jonathan for your preteen. You might also wish to share this book with other moms in a Moms' Support Group. Chapter 14 tells you how to begin such a group and provides a complete study guide for a support group. All the details are taken care of; all you need to do is to get some moms together for coffee and propose the idea.

This Road Has a Destination

I've recently had thoughts like, *Isn't it great? Our guys seem to be on the right track. Soon it'll be smooth sailing. Before we realize it, the last one will be gone from the nest and the honeymoon will begin again.*

My daydreams were interrupted by a dear friend who is well into the empty nest. She reminded me that grown children come with daughters-in-law and grandchildren and the family just gets larger and larger. There are even more opportunities to trust each other and God and more opportunities to stay humble.

As I reflected on her comments, I saw that she was right. I challenge each of us as we continue down the roads of our lives to stop to pick the flowers along the way. Enjoy each unique and developing preteen and teen. Hold onto the moments of love. Stop fearing the future or pulling up the plant to examine the roots. Instead enjoy the good times and look toward a wonderful future, which will not be perfect but will be shared with adult children who love and respect their parents.

It's the relationship that counts. Today. Tomorrow. And forever.

EXERCISE 10

Relax! Who Me?

I. Think of areas that you feel responsible for but can't control. Turn them over to the Lord each night before you go to sleep.

1.

2.

3.

II. What interests do you have outside the home? If none, list something to pursue.

1.

2.

3.

III. What can you do this week to build your relationship with your mate?

1.

2.

3.

IV. Copy the Hensley Grid and follow yourself around for a week. Then take a critical look at how you spend your time. Can you swap some activities for a time of rest and relaxation?

V. List several ideas that might add humor to your relationship with your preteen or teen.

1.

2.

3.

VI. Go on and relax. Yes, you!

PART SIX

Guidelines

Chapter Thirteen

HOW TO MAKE YOUR
PARENTS YOUR FRIENDS
By Jonathan Arp

Are you looking forward to your teenage years? Maybe you are eleven or twelve or even thirteen, and you're wondering what lies ahead. Let me introduce myself. I'm Jonathan Arp, and I'm fourteen. My mother is the author of the book your mom's been reading. I have two older brothers, so my mom and dad have lots of experience with teenagers. Most of the time we get along great with our parents. I'd like to tell you some of the things we have discovered, which are making these years fun.

What are your dreams and goals for your teenage years? I bet some of the goals on your list match those on mine:

1. Learning to drive
2. Being taller than my dad
3. Choosing my own music, clothes, hair style
4. Dating and girls
5. Having a part-time job and making lots of money

How about it? Is your list similar to mine? We'll both be able to accomplish our goals better if we build a good relationship with our parents.

Look at it this way. If we have a good relationship with our parents, we'll have more freedom and get to do more things. Our teen years will be more fun.

WHAT ARE MOTHERS LIKE?

I've learned that my mom really cares about me. I'm also sure your mother cares about you and wants your teenage years to be the best ever. She wouldn't be reading this book if she didn't.

I don't know your mom personally so I don't know what her personality is like, what she looks like, or how she cooks. But all moms are alike in some ways. For instance, all mothers thrive on appreciation. When your mom cooks a nice dinner, she likes to hear about it. A hug now and then can make her day.

It's hard work being a mom so I try to thank my mom when she does something special for me. Sometimes I try to do something special for her, especially on her birthday and Mother's Day. If I don't have any money, I write her a note or make her a coupon book, filled with coupons to redeem for my services, like taking out the trash and cleaning the kitchen.

Believe it or not, my older brother Jarrett tells me that moms are affected by peer pressure, just as we are. They want to be liked and admired by their friends. Every once in a while they won't let us do something merely because of pressure from other parents.

WHAT ARE DADS LIKE?

Just like moms, no two dads are exactly the same, although they share certain characteristics. First, I think dads, like mothers, enjoy being appreciated. They also want our respect. They want us to recognize them as boss, the guy who works hard to support the family.

The peculiar thing about dads is the way they express their love for us. Some dads spend a lot of time with their kids. My dad takes me to breakfast every once in a while before school. Sometimes he plays tennis with me or we go camping together.

Some fathers, however, are much different. They express their love by buying us skiing equipment or encouraging us in a sport or activity. Other dads are big teases. I know a teenage girl whose dad calls her "Fat Baby" and always teases her about her weight. (When she was younger, he called her "Miss Piggy.")

This girl, Heidi, gets tired of the teasing, but she intuitively knows it's her dad's way of showing his love for her. When he was in the hospital for heart surgery, she'd walk into his room and say, "Hey, Dad, it's me, your Fat Baby! I'm going to come and sit on your lap if you don't smile. You wouldn't want all that weight on you, would you, Dad?"

Her dad would make a fake grimace and break out laughing.

We need to recognize our own dad's way of showing his love to us, as odd as it may be, so we can appreciate it.

BUILDING A FRIENDSHIP

So how can we make these parents our friends? I've watched my brothers, and they talk to my parents just as they do the guys on their soccer teams. Instead of just asking for lunch money, they sit down and talk to Mom and Dad about what happens at school. So do I.

Parents are really interested in what we're doing even though they sometimes seem too busy to listen. My brothers gave me some advice when I was almost thirteen: "Mom and Dad will be less scared of the teen years if you let them know what you're thinking," they said.

Years ago my dad began saying, "Our family's a team. We're committed to each member of the family, just as the goalie of the soccer team has to cooperate with the sweeper. The team won't win if the members don't work together."

This idea has worked well in our family. My older brothers and I all play soccer so it is easy for us to apply team principles to our family. In soccer each player must be committed to work with the other players. It's the same in a family. If you don't work together, everybody will lose in the end.

Is your family a team? If not, what can you do to change the situation? You may groan and think it's hopeless.

But it's not. I've learned a few tips from my brothers that I'd like to pass along to you.

Give Your Parents Reason to Trust You.

Your parents may not be as excited about your teenage years as you are. It's likely they have been scared by their older friends' horror stories about rebellious teenagers and problems like drugs and drinking. You can help change their outlook in your preteen years by letting them know you can be trusted.

You're probably wondering, *How do I do that?* My brothers gave me a hint. "When Mom and Dad give you certain responsibilities and privileges," they said, "watch how you handle them. Try not to take advantage of the privileges."

Take my curfew, for example. I try to be at home on time. If I'm going to be late one night, I take time to call home and let Mom and Dad know I'm going to be late. This year my curfew was changed from 10:00 to 10:30, because my parents felt they could trust me.

Talk to Your Parents about Your Music.

When I was twelve, my parents and I talked about the music I listened to. They told me how loud it seemed to them and how much some of the lyrics went against their morals.

I agreed with them. "The important thing to me," I said, "is the lyrics. I ask myself, *What do they say?* If I don't like the message, I don't buy the record."

It had never occurred to my parents that I had some guidelines for choosing my music or that, believe it or not, my standards were not all that different from theirs. After this conversation, they stopped hassling me about my music.

What if I had taken the other approach and said, "I'm going to listen to what I want to and it is none of your business!"? The discussion would have ended in a fight.

Along this same line, remember to tolerate your parents' music. I'm not any fonder of "elevator music" than you are, but I've learned it's a two-way street. They really enjoy that mellow sound!

This principle of give-and-take also works for fads like long hair and "far-out" clothes. My brother, Joel, wanted to have long hair during his senior year in high school. He was co-captain of the soccer team and most of the players had their hair long in back.

I was surprised when Mom and Dad allowed Joel to keep his hair longer than they liked.

After soccer season was over, Joel got his hair cut. "I don't want my appearance to influence my getting accepted to college. Sometimes the interviewers think like Mom and Dad," he explained when I asked the reason for his sudden change.

Learn to Laugh with Your Parents, Not at Them.

As preteens and teens, we're used to sarcasm. We can't escape it at school, and we often practice it at home so we can readily make a good comeback.

I've learned that parents feel threatened when we throw sarcastic remarks at them. They think we're putting them down. Nothing destroys my relationship with my mom more than a remark like "You wouldn't understand; you're too old."

Laughing together, however, builds up the relationship. So share the funny incidents that happen at school with your parents.

We laugh a lot in our family. Sometimes it's really dumb things, like the day my dad opened the lid of the trash can and pieces of chicken fell all over my mom's newly waxed floor.

"The trash can just threw up!" he said.

My dad and mom are always doing silly things. One summer, when Jarrett was in college, he and Joel got to stay alone for two weeks. Dad sent them a sympathy card with this note: "We know how hard it is to be without your parents. You have our deepest sympathy."

Prepare for the Emotional and Physical Changes Ahead.

You might be wondering about how your body will change. I've found that it helps to know what's coming. My mom gave me a set of tapes by Dr. James Dobson called "Preparing for Adolescence."

Dr. Dobson gives tips in these tapes to help us resist peer pressure. You might want to ask your mom to get the tapes and the workbook that goes with them for you.

THE TEENAGE CHALLENGE

About six months before my thirteenth birthday, my parents said to me, "We want to prepare you for your teen years by giving you a Teenage Challenge. The challenge will include achievement in four different areas: physical, intellectual, spiritual, and practical.

"We'd like you to think about how you would like to grow in each of these areas. Then we will sit down together and write the challenge. If you complete it by your thirteenth birthday, you will receive a reward."

Mom and Dad and I agreed on the following Teenage Challenge:

I. Physical Goals
   A. Run one mile in under eight minutes.
   B. Learn to play a good game of tennis: work on serve, forehand, and backhand.

II. Intellectual Goals
   A. Read one missionary biography and write a report.

III. Spiritual Goals
   A. Work out your own standards and convictions for

your teenage years. Do a Code of Conduct Bible Study and a Study of Proverbs to see God's view of habits such as laziness, pride, cheating, and lying. [These studies can be found in the appendices in Dillow and Arp's *Sanity in the Summertime* (Nashville: Thomas Nelson Publishers, Inc., 1981).]
  B. Memorize Psalm 1.

IV. Practical Goals
  A. Earn $35.00. We will match what you save before your birthday.
  B. Plan and execute an overnight campout with Dad.

Doing this challenge helped me make decisions about my standards before I became a teenager. For instance, I made a commitment always to tell the truth and thought about a lot of the issues—drinking, drugs, sex—before I became a teenager.

The physical part of my challenge was the most fun. I took a tennis clinic over the summer, which helped me a lot, and played tennis almost every day. At the end of that summer, I was selected as the most improved player for that clinic. I won a Prince Pro tennis racket!

If your parents give you a Teenage Challenge, let me encourage you to do it. It will be fun and you and your parents will work through potential problems ahead of time.

Your teenage years will be lots easier if you have a good family team. Remember, you want to be a strong team player. I read somewhere that the average player runs as much as eight miles in just one soccer game. It takes a lot of work, and you've got to be in shape.

Getting ready to be a teenager is a lot like a soccer game. You need to get in shape by building a good relationship with your parents and preparing for those eight years. It'll be a tough game at best, but you can win. I know because we're winning at my house.

Chapter Fourteen

LEADER'S GUIDE
FOR SUPPORT GROUPS
By Kris Tomasik

Welcome to *Almost 13*! Over the coming weeks, you will be leading a Moms' Support Group, using *Almost 13* as your textbook. Together, you and the group members will build a loving, caring community. You'll share stories with each other about your experiences of mothering, and your hopes, fears, and dreams as you look forward to your young person's growing up. You'll laugh together. You'll cry together. You'll get encouraged together. And most of all, you'll discover that *nobody* has it all together. It's O.K. to be on the way.

What is a "Moms' Support Group?" To understand, let's look briefly at each of the words.

Moms: You are all mothers. You have all undertaken the sometimes awesome, sometimes thankless, but ever present job of mothering. The idealized myth of the perfect supermom is causing many of us ordinary, human women to begin to crack under the strain. In this group we'll strive for a balanced, biblical view of motherhood, and of ourselves in that role.

Support: With so much negative peer pressure from the culture around us, we need each other's support as we tackle the job of mothering. *Support* means love and acceptance, not criticizing nor judging nor sneering nor holding aloof. It means we come together, just as we are, and we care for each other, much as the Holy Spirit cares for us. We don't break confidence about what is shared in the group, and we don't talk outside of the group about what went on inside the group.

Kris Tomasik is a former junior high and high school Curriculum Managing Editor for David C. Cook Publishing Co.

Group: This is a group, a living organism, similar to that which St. Paul described as the body of Christ. Every member is equally important, and the "leader", who only serves as facilitator, is as much a part of the group as any other member. This kind of group-centered leader trusts the group's capacity to solve its own problems. She knows that the group as a whole is smarter than any one member including herself. She realizes that a decision arrived at by all the group members is usually the best for the total group. She believes in the combined wisdom of the group and in the group process.

To help create the caring, protective Moms' Support Group environment described above, the following Moms' Support Group Contract was developed to be used in Week One. Asking each member to read carefully and to sign a group contract insures mutual respect and confidentiality, thus starting the support group on a positive and relaxed basis.

Starting the Moms' Support Group

You can begin by calling a friend and sharing the idea with her. Together you could call other friends and maybe even have a coffee to discuss the idea.

A support group can be you and one other friend or it can be as large as six to eight moms. A group that is too large cannot function effectively unless it breaks down into smaller units. The group can meet weekly or monthly. Some groups meet in the morning, others meet for lunch, and others in the afternoon. Choose a time when each of you is free for a couple of hours so no one feels rushed and under pressure.

The study guide which follows is broken into twelve weeks, which can be used once a month for a year or used weekly to get moms' group going. You can rotate leadership each session or one person can take the responsibility.

MOMS' SUPPORT GROUP CONTRACT

As a member of this Moms' Support Group, I understand that I will be expected to:

1. Read the assigned chapter(s) and do the chapter exercises to the best of my time and ability.
2. Be regular and on time.
3. Listen with compassion and an open mind to others.
4. Avoid giving advice to others unless they ask for it; never criticize or condemn.
5. Take responsibility for my own situation only, not anyone else's.
6. Keep confidentiality. Outside of the group, I will not discuss with anyone, including other group members, anything that went on in the group. I may, of course, discuss with my spouse and other family members things that pertain strictly to me and to us. I may discuss with anyone things that pertain strictly to me.

I have read the above carefully, and I understand and agree to these guidelines.

(Signed) _____

You can begin any time of the year. Many groups begin in the fall, once the children are back in school.

You will want to send out information to prospective moms of preteens and teens. Distributing a low-cost mailer or brochure can help spark enthusiasm and attendance for a Moms' Support Group. Include the following information:

Purpose: The Moms' Support Group is a program for mothers of preteens. In this high-stress period of a mother's life she often feels inadequate, frustrated, and lonely. Frequently these feelings go unresolved. A Moms' support group will help meet the significant needs of mothers by:

- providing for the development of close, supportive friendship
- discussing specific skills for positive parenting
- building a sense of personal worth in the mother
- promoting spiritual growth and commitment to Jesus Christ

Format: Moms' Support Group sessions are times of encouraging one another and learning how to "regroup, relate, release, and relax." As we become involved in giving and receiving support and encouragement, we are better able to keep our perspective. The emphasis of the group is on building our relationship with our offspring. The group is a time of positive mutual reinforcement.

Resource: The Moms' Support Group uses as its text *Almost 13* by Claudia Arp, the mother of three teenage sons who, with her husband Dave, conducts seminars on marriage and family.

Also include cost, time, location, nursery facilities, and a registration blank.

Ways of Learning

Throughout this study guide you'll find several ways of learning suggested:

Sharing stories: It is important for women to share their "stories" with each other. The act of presenting her own personal experience both clarifies and validates it for a woman, and hearing other women's stories helps her discover, "Hey! I'm not alone!"

Discussion: True discussion involves all the participants and is not a monologue by the leader or one dominant group member. A discussion leader's main function is to ensure democratic participation by drawing quiet ones out ("Mary, what do you think about this?") and by quelling overtalkative others ("Thanks for your ideas, Joan. What do some of the rest of you feel?").

Role playing: It's one thing to talk about a situation and another actually to experience it. Role play gives participants a chance to relive the feelings of a situation in a safe environment with objective observers. By switching roles, a mother can also put herself in the other person's shoes, an invaluable aid to empathy.

The ideal group size for these activities is four people each for story-sharing and role-playing with eight taking part in a discussion. Any exceptions to these numbers will be noted in the study. If you know your Moms' Support Group will exceed more than eight people, you'll want to recruit leaders for small groups and train them in the group-centered style of leadership described above.

Here are some ways that Moms in support groups have said the group helped them:

1. I've discovered that I'm not alone.

2. I've learned that much of what my husband and I are going through with our teens is normal.

3. I've gotten to know other moms and moms of friends of my preteen.

4. As a group of moms, we agreed on some standards such as: curfew and what places are off-limits for our preteens and teens. Our preteens did not feel as much peer pressure once we moms agreed on some ground rules.

The difference between reading a book and having it affect your life is involvement! Being a part of a Moms' Support Group will help you make a change and make progress.

Isn't there someone you want to call right now and begin to organize your own Moms' Support Group? You and your teen will be the winners!

Week 1: What Is a Mother?

Based on chapter 1

> *Goals*: To introduce group members to each other and to the Moms' Support Group.
> To define our expectations of ourselves as mothers.

Content summary: All women experience subtle yet definite pressures to be a certain kind of mother. Some of these expectations are helpful; others are unrealistic and damaging. Especially as a woman enters the high-stress period of her children's adolescence years, she needs to develop realistic expectations of herself, to cultivate caring, supportive friendships with other women, and to find her ultimate worth in her relationship with Jesus.

You'll need: Copies of *Almost 13*, by Claudia Arp; copies of Group Contract for all present; paper, pencils, and Bibles.

ACTIVITY 1 – INTRODUCTION TO A MOMS' SUPPORT GROUP (10 minutes)

Introduce the idea of a Moms' Support Group by briefly defining each of the words. Use the ideas from the introduction to this leader's guide.

Distribute copies of the Group Contract and ask members to read carefully and sign. Answer questions about the guidelines. Number 5, for example, is designed to free members from the compulsion of "rescuing" other members and to encourage personal, individual responsibility. Number 6, confidentiality, is designed to prevent the destructive "triangling" that can occur when two people get together and talk about an absent third party.

Show and distribute copies of the book *Almost 13* by Claudia Arp. Read together from Chapter 1 the sections headed "Learning to Relate," "Building to Release," and "Starting to Relax" to give the women an idea of the direction of the book and the group.

ACTIVITY 2–STORY-SHARING: GROWING MEMORIES (40 minutes)

This activity will help members get acquainted with each other by telling the stories of their lives so far with their preteens.

Have women break into groups of four. For a seven-minute time period the women are to recall memories about their preteens. This means each woman will have about one and one half minutes to share. Call time so the groups can break up and reform into new groups of four for another seven-minute story-telling segment. There will be four of these seven-minute segments, so your total story-sharing time should run about thirty minutes.

Here are the four story-sharing topics. Call these out at the seven-minute intervals:

- Share a story about your preteen's birth.
- Share a story about you and your preteen at age two.
- Share a story about you and your preteen at ages seven to ten.
- Share a story about you and your preteen now.

At the end of the story-sharing time, ask women to take five to ten minutes for personal reflection. They may want to jot down some thoughts in answer to these questions, or they may simply think about them:

1. What makes my preteen so special to me?
2. Where have we been in our relationship, and where are we now?
3. What is the greatest need in my relationship with my preteen right now?

ACTIVITY 3 – WHAT IS A MOTHER? (20 minutes)

Give women paper and pencil and distribute Bibles. Ask them to take five minutes to write their gut-level answers to these three open-ended questions. (You may want to write the questions on a large sheet of paper ahead of time.)

1. I think a mother is...
2. Society says a mother is...
3. The Bible says motherhood is...

For fifteen minutes discuss possible answers to these questions. There are really no right or wrong answers, even number 3 is open to some interpretation. The point of this activity is to help women become aware of the expectations they place on the idea of motherhood and to think about whether they want to continue holding those, or whether they may want to revamp some of their thinking.

Ideas you may want to bring out are:

• We inherit some of our ideas about motherhood from our own mothers, but these may or may not be the way we ultimately choose to do our mothering ourselves.

• Society loads us with all kinds of notions about motherhood, from the saintly all-sacrificing martyr to the overachieving supermom. Many segments of society devalue motherhood altogether.

• Although some religious people tend to glorify motherhood to the point almost of deifying it, the Bible does not. However the Bible does value motherhood and the family as a whole (Hebrews 13:4; Titus 2:4,5; numerous passages on familial love, including Ephesians 5:21-6:4), but it does not point to motherhood as the totality of a woman's existence. Instead, as Jesus tells Martha, "But one thing is needed, and Mary has chosen that good part, which will not be taken away from her" (Luke 10:42). What had Mary chosen? Not to fuss over the household, as Martha had. Not a career, either. Mary had chosen to sit at the feet of Jesus.

To close, ask women to contemplate silently on this thought: *In what ways do I need more to "sit at Jesus' feet?"* *Homework*: Do exercise 1 in chapter 2, "Will the Well-rounded Teenager Please Stand Up?"

Week 2: Personality Profiles—and Problems

Based on chapter 2

> Goals: To help mothers understand their own and their preteen's basic personality temperament and focus on the strengths of each.

Content summary: The means of categorizing personality types abound today, but each shows us a basic truth: each individual is different. Different does not necessarily have to be "wrong"—it may just be different. As moms look at their preteens in light of one such system, they can begin to breathe a sigh of relief and see that God has simply used a different blueprint on different people.

You'll need: Role-playing suggestions for Activity 4 in the study guide, and copies of *Almost 13* with exercise 2 for homework assignment. Save exercise 2 for later use.

ACTIVITY 1 – PERSONALITY PROFILES (10 minutes)

Briefly review the four personality types the book discusses: *sanguine* (Sally Sparkle), *choleric* (Take-charge Thomas), *phlegmatic* (Laid-back Larry), and *melancholic* (Roller-coaster Rene). Point out that this ancient system of understanding personality dates back to the Greek physician Hippocrates (who lived around 400 B.C.), but was recently popularized by Tim LaHaye in his book *Spirit-Controlled Temperament* (Tyndale House Publishers, 1968).

Ask group members to mention any other systems of personality analysis they're familiar with. Some that might be mentioned include the D-I-S-C four-fold profile developed by Personal Dynamics Institute, the four types being dominant, *influencing*, *steady*, and *compliant*. There is also the more complicated but more finely tuned Myers-Briggs Type Indicator developed by Isabel Briggs Myers. It classifies people according to four polarities, introvert or extrovert, sensing or intuitive, thinking or feeling, judgment or perception.

Briefly discuss:

• What is the value of seeing others in terms of a personality profile?

• What are the dangers?

ACTIVITY 2 – PERSONALIZING THE PERSONALITIES (15 minutes)

Participants will be reviewing their homework by doing this activity, as well as by sharing their stories. Those who haven't yet completed the Understanding Our Strengths and Weaknesses exercise for their preteen and for themselves will have a chance to consider it.

Divide into groups of four for story-sharing and ask each woman to share two stories: one that illustrates her preteen's personality type with its attending strengths and weaknesses, and one that illustrates hers. As they share, the story-tellers should not divulge the personality type they are describing but should leave it to group members to guess.

ACTIVITY 3 – WHO NEEDS WHAT? (10 minutes)

In groups of eight, quickly discuss two questions:

1. What kind of parenting does each of the personality types need? (What parenting style will most motivate this preteen?)

2. Which mom/preteen personality types might have the hardest time getting along? The easiest? Why?

In answer to question 1, one group suggested these ideas: a phlegmatic preteen may need a "cheerleader" style of parenting; a melancholic needs encouragement because she's already too hard on herself; a choleric needs suggestions and reasoning—the worst approach would be rigidity with direct orders; a sanguine needs a solid base of unwavering approval.

In answer to question 2, one group saw potential conflict between a melancholic mom expecting perfection of a sanguine daughter who just wants to "have fun," or between a "take charge" mom and a "take charge" son who might get into a battle of wills.

ACTIVITY 4—PERSONALITY TYPE ROLE PLAYS (25 minutes)

A word about role play:

A role play is simply acting out a short skit in which people simulate a real or imaginary situation. It gives the players a chance to relive the feelings of the situation in a safe environment and to practice better ways of relating. Dramatic ability is not required. Simply live out the situation for a minute or two or until inspiration runs out, then stop and debrief.

Briefly explain role playing to your participants. Then have them divide into groups of four and act out the following situations twice. The first time the players should emphasize only the weaknesses of the personality type; the second time they should try to utilize the strengths of that type. Since each situation calls for only two players, the other two members of the group should serve as observers, giving the players feedback and helping them debrief their feelings about the action.

Here are the situations:

• A choleric mom tries to get her phlegmatic son to clean his room.

• A melancholic mom and a melancholic daughter are both having their periods at the same time.

• A phlegmatic mom tries to show her sanguine daughter that the daughter's friends are having a bad influence on her.

• Choose a situation from your own experience as mom of your preteen.

Each person should have a chance to participate in the last situation so you may wish to use only one of the simulations as a warm-up, going directly to the actual one.

When three to four minutes remain, discuss the experience as a whole group by asking:

• What did you learn about your preteen by doing these role plays?

• About yourself?

Homework: Exercise 2 in chapter 3, "No Strings Attached."

Week 3: Unconditional Love

Based on chapter 3

Goal: To help participants experience God's unconditional love and forgiveness and therefore be enabled to give it.

Content summary: God's unconditional love and forgiveness are a model for all parental love. But unless we have experienced that love ourselves, we will be crippled in our ability to give it. We can receive it, though, by simply opening ourselves to its healing power.

You'll need: Each participant's own completed homework, "Accepting Your Preteen," paper, pencils, copies of *Almost 13*, with exercise 3 for homework.

ACTIVITY 1 – HOW AM I LIKE MY PRETEEN? (10 minutes)

Ask everyone to take a look at her homework, "Accepting Your Preteen." Explain that often the reason our preteens' faults aggravate us so much is that *we have the same ones*. Before we can accept and forgive our child, we need to accept and forgive ourselves. To do that, we need to have the courage to look at ourselves.

Ask participants to add a fourth column to the sheet: *Ways I see this fault of my preteen in myself.*

For example, the book cites as an example of a preteen's fault a "smart mouth." The mother's wrong response is to "snap back, criticize, and give lecture no. 309." Isn't that the same thing as a "smart mouth" on an adult level?

Allow everyone personal time to write.

ACTIVITY 2 – BASKING IN GOD'S LOVE (15 minutes)

"I have found that the extent to which I am picking on my preteen is the extent to which I am picking on and hating myself," remarked one woman. "And I do all of the above when I am not letting myself experience God's overwhelming love for me."

Ask participants to settle back comfortably in their chairs and even close their eyes if they wish. Invite them to become perfectly relaxed and to imagine that God's love is a warming, healing light beaming down on them. Invite them to imagine that what you are about to read is God speaking directly to them. Then read with warmth and love this poem:

LOVE LETTER FROM GOD

My child, my precious child,
I will take care of you.
I am to be your only concern.
Listen to me.
Abide in my love.
Go and be yourself.
I will show you the way.
I will always love you.
I will always be here for you.
Bring my love to others
Just by being you.

By Tish Murphy

When you're finished, invite participants to continue to sit quietly, basking in God's love for a few minutes more. They should listen for God's words of acceptance of them as they strive to rid themselves of their faults.

ACTIVITY 3 – EXPERIENCING FORGIVENESS (10 minutes)

Give each woman a clean sheet of paper and ask her to write down anything that she would like to ask for God's forgiveness. Tell the group that this information is personal and they will not be sharing their list with the other mothers in the group. This activity is just between them and God. They can include their wrong reactions and the faults they have discovered in their relating to their preteen or teen.

When everyone is finished, have the women copy this verse from 1 John 1:9 across the page: "If we confess our sins, He is faithful and just to forgive us our sins and to cleanse us from all unrighteousness."

Stress that we are forgiven completely. When we confess our known sins, God forgives us also for the ones we don't know.

Then have the women rip their papers into tiny pieces and throw them away. Give assurance that they are forgiven and it is a new day!

ACTIVITY 4 – RELATIONSHIP ROLE PLAYS (15 minutes)

As *Almost 13* suggests, sometimes it is not enough to forgive the preteen. Sometimes it is necessary to seek actively his or her forgiveness for wrongs we have done.

Divide into groups of four and have the women role-play situations in which a mother must ask her preteen's forgiveness. Encourage the women to use actual situations from their experience and to keep the focus on the *asking*. *Actually asking* someone's forgiveness is not as easy as it sounds! Everyone needs practice and role playing is a good way to get it. Role-players should strive for a straight apology, one that states the facts of the apologizer's wrongdoing and simply asks for forgiveness. There must be no need to get jabs in at the kid, no need to gush, or bewail how horrible the apologizer is.

As always, the group members not doing the role play should act as observers and give feedback. They should be on the lookout especially for any hidden digs and overly self-deprecating apologies, i.e., apologies that are not "straight."

At the end of the role-play time, discuss briefly as a whole group:

- Why is it so hard to apologize?
- Why is it so hard to apologize to one's preteen?

ACTIVITY 5 – PASSING THE POSITIVES (10 minutes)

Now that the women have done some work on accepting and forgiving themselves and their preteens, they are ready to look at the positives.

Regroup as for Activity 3, but this time you will be passing the positives. The first mother names some outstanding quality of her preteen to the woman on her right. That woman names back to the mother some outstanding quality the woman sees in the mother. Continue around the circle once; then reverse and go around the circle again.

Close by thanking God for loving us in all our humanness, in our strengths and weaknesses, and pray for His help in living out His kind of love to our families.

Homework: Exercise 3 in chapter 4, "Birdlegs, Braces, and Zits."

Week 4: Praise Them, Praise Them

Based on book chapter 4

Goals: To help mothers learn how and why to give preteens genuine praise.

Content summary: Early adolescence is one of the

most fragile times of a person's life. Parents need to be sensitive to this age range, and to develop good habits of genuine encouragement.

You'll need: Each woman's copy of *Almost 13,* construction paper, felt tip markers, pencils, old magazines, glue, scissors, exercise 4 for homework.

ACTIVITY 1 – MANY MEMORIES (20 minutes)

Read this quotation from Dr. Urie Bronfenbrenner, eminent authority on child development from Cornell University: "The junior high years are probably the most critical to the development of a child's mental health. During this period of self-doubt, the personality is often assaulted and damaged beyond repair."[1] Today we are going to share some memories from our own early adolescence in order to help us gain empathy with our preteens. Perhaps some unhappy memories will come up. If so, this can be an important part of our own healing. In their book *Five Cries of Parents,* Merton and Irene Strommen make the point that "our past experiences and decisions profoundly affect our present perceptions as parent."[2] Clearing up our own wounded memories of our early years of adolescence can help us deal from a place of wholeness with our preteens.

Begin by praying that the Holy Spirit will be present as you share memories and will bring comfort and healing to each as needed.

Then divide into groups of four for story-sharing. Ask each participant to respond to these two situations:

• It's dinnertime with your family and you are twelve years old. What's happening?

• You're age thirteen and you're in the most traumatic place for you. Where is that, and why?

End this activity by giving women a few moments to consider silently where, if at all, they need further healing of their own preteen memories.

ACTIVITY 2 – ROLE-PLAY PRAISE (20 minutes)

You can.see why preteens and teens need a lot of encouragement! Self-esteem is hardly at a lower ebb than in the junior high years. As *Almost 13* points out, it takes FOUR positive comments to counteract ONE negative one. We all need practice in praising.

Divide into groups of four to do praise role plays. Using situations from their own lives with their preteens, role-players should first act out how not to do it, then re-enact the same situation giving genuine, sincere, verbal praise.

Be sure to cover these four "how-not-to-do-its":
- Gushy, insincere flattery
- Mixed compliment, with hidden jabs
- Embarrassing-to-teen compliment
- "Guesswork" compliment, totally nonverbal "hints"
- "Bait" compliment, compliment as prelude to criticism ("You're such a smart girl, BUT...")

ACTIVITY 3 – PRAISE PARTNER PROJECTS (20 minutes)

Refer women to the suggested praise projects listed in chapter 4 of the textbook. Ask for group brainstorming to come up with other such projects, ones they've done, heard of, or had done to them!

Then have the women choose praise project partners, take the art supplies available, and turn them loose either to begin or to plan their praise projects. For instance, some mothers may choose to make the Thanksgiving Acrostics. They could cut out letters and pictures from the old magazines to make a snappy looking, yet inexpensive, piece of artwork. Others may decide to give a special person party and begin to plan it. Others may take time to write a special letter.

Five minutes before time is up, have the partners form a contract with each other to reinforce their assignment from last week. Since it takes three weeks to develop a new habit, partners should contract to help each other remember to continue "Building Up Your Preteen" for the next two weeks. Perhaps they will want to schedule times to call and remind each other. Perhaps they will want to have coffee and compare notes at the end of the week. In some way they should make themselves accountable to one another for the next two weeks.

Homework: Exercise 4 in chapter 5, "Getting Off the Lecture Circuit."

Week 5: Please Listen To Me

Based on book chapter 5

Goals: To help women identify and correct common listening errors, and learn the skills of active, empathic listening.

Content summary: To listen is to love. Yet truly listening to someone, especially a preteen, is hard to do. We can avoid the common listening pitfalls of interrupting, lecturing, acting shocked, judging, etc., by learning to "listen with the heart."

You'll need: Large sheet of butcher paper, marker, paper, pencils, copies of *Almost 13*, exercise 5 for homework.

ACTIVITY 1 – ROLE-PLAY SWITCHES (20 minutes)

There are many types of listening mistakes. In their book *I Need to Have You Know Me*, Roland and Doris Larson describe three such mistakes: *listening with half an ear* (the other half of mother's ear and mind are concentrating on getting supper); "*Yes, but*" *listening* (mother interrupts and tells the preteen what she *should* have done); "*I can top that*" *listening* (mother's sob story from the past is bigger and better than the preteen's).[3]

Post a large sheet of butcher paper and ask women to brainstorm other kinds of listening blunders based on their own experience and the ideas in *Almost 13*.

Your group's list of listening mistakes might look like this:

- half listening
- interrupting with irrelevancy
- lecturing, condemning, or scolding
- reacting with shock ("Gasp! How could you?!")
- giving advice—trying to solve the preteen's problem for her

Divide the women into groups of two to role-play role switches. One player should be the mother who is a poor listener, the other being the preteen who needs to talk. The players should switch roles every other scene until they have completed four role-plays. In each, the "poor listener" should deliberately make one of the listening errors listed. The woman playing the person needing to talk should speak about something that actually is bothering her now in real life.

Players may use situations from their own experience or ones like these:

- A preteen tries to tell her mother about a fight she had with her best friend while mother is making dinner.

- A preteen tries to tell her mother she has doubts about whether the Bible is really true.

- A preteen is trying to decide whether or not to go to a school dance (or some other "gray area") and would like to air his thinking.

With several minutes remaining in the allotted time, ask players to debrief in groups of four to six by considering these questions:

- How did it feel not to be listened to?
- What kind of being shut out or cut off felt worst to you? What kind do you think feels worst to your preteen?
- What would you identify as your most common listening error?

ACTIVITY 2 – LISTENING WITH THE HEART (20 minutes)

What constitutes good listening? "The first essential in listening is to convey an attitude of warm interest, free from a spirit of judgment or criticism," say Christian researchers Merton and Irene Strommen in their book, *Five Cries of Parents*.[4] Educator Barbara Varenhorst calls it "listening with your heart."[5]

What else constitutes good listening? Ask your group to brainstorm specific ideas from their experience and from *Almost 13*. These additional ideas, condensed from *Five Cries of Parents*, may help as you brainstorm:

Guide 1: Listen in ways that encourage expression of feelings.

• Give affirming responses, such as "I can understand what you're saying," or "I can appreciate your willingness to tell me that."

• Use general leads instead of specific questions: "Mind telling me about your game today?" or "Would you care to explain that more fully?" or "Could you give me a 'for instance?' "

Guide 2: Listen to discern the adolescent's perspective.

• Use feedback responses to show that you are trying to understand what is being said: "Let me tell you what I am hearing, to see if I am on target," or "In other words, you....Does that sound right?"

• Use clarification responses to listen for the feelings expressed behind the words, such as, "You resent Dad's absence from your games. Is that correct?" or "You feel we're picking on you. Is that it?"

Divide the women into groups of four to practice the good listening they have just described. Stress that they should particularly listen for feelings. They may want to use the same situations they just role-played.

When time is almost up, have the small groups debrief with these questions:

- How does it feel to be listened to?
- Why does real listening show real caring?
- Who do you have in your life who really listens to you?

ACTIVITY 3 – LISTENING NEEDS (20 minutes)

In order to be good listeners to our preteens, we must have our own listening needs met. If we are just bursting with all the things *we* need to say, it will be impossible for us to be good listeners. We can fail to get our own listening needs met in two ways: by not talking because we don't have adequate supportive friendships, or by talking to the wrong people, who are themselves incapable of listening to us.

So we need to get our own listening needs met first. Then, as *Almost 13* points out, we need to make sure we have enough *communication places* and *communication activities* for interaction to take place with our preteen.

Have the women choose partners. Distribute paper and pencils and ask them to spend the remainder of this session analyzing and finding solutions to these three questions:

1. Am I getting my own listening needs met?
2. Is there a comfortable communication place in our home?
3. Do I share enough communication activities with my preteen?

For example, if a woman realized there was no comfortable communication center in her home, she might draw a rough scale model of her living room or den and rearrange the furniture to make it more suitable to conversation.

Close by thanking God, the God who communicates, for the way He listens to us.

Homework: Exercise 5 in chapter 6, "Rebuilding the Communication Bridge."

Week 6: Saying No and Expressing Anger

Based on book chapter 6

> *Goals*: To help women feel comfortable and gain skills in saying no and in expressing their anger appropriately.

Content summary: This chapter deals with what may well be contemporary women's greatest bugbears: being assertive enough to say No, and strong enough to express her anger appropriately. By looking at the example of Jesus, women can gain the courage to learn the skills of strength.

You'll need: Bibles, paper, pencils, the Anger Ladder from chapter 6, plus exercises 6 and 7 for homework.

ACTIVITY 1 – IN HIS STEPS (15 minutes)

Point out that the chapter for this week deals with what are perhaps the hardest behaviors for women to act out effectively: saying no (giving a reprimand) and expressing anger. We can only overcome our tremendous inner resistance to these tasks with the help of our Savior and by following His example.

Divide women into discussion groups of eight. Ask them to read the story of Jesus and the money changers in Mark 11:15-19 and to consider these two questions:

• What can I learn from this passage about anger?

• What can I learn from this passage about saying no?

After groups have had a chance to consider, call for brief summary sharing. Some thoughts the groups might come up with are these:

• Some situations rightly provoke us to anger and to corrective action.

• We will not necessarily be popular with those whom we correct.

• Anger and assertive action are not in and of themselves wrong, but are part of the model that Jesus set for *all* Christians to follow.

Point out that Jesus' action is a strong example. We will not want to rush into our preteen's room tomorrow and "overthrow" his "moneytables." But this example was chosen precisely because we so often fear and name as "unchristian" this strong side of our personalities.

Briefly discuss: Why do you think women often hesitate to express their anger or to give reprimands?

ACTIVITY 2 – THE ANGER LADDER (10 minutes)

Point out that expressing anger is rough because it means risking not being liked, which is extremely unpleasant for those of us who have been schooled to be "nice" and have everybody like us. It's so unpleasant, in fact, that we may not even have the words to use to express our anger appropriately. Therefore we either go to the extreme of blowing up, or we remain silent, all the while seething inside. Note that on the Anger Ladder described in this chapter of *Almost 13*, "silent seething" is really "passive-aggressive" behavior, the lowest possible rung. Even the person who blows up is higher up the ladder!

Ask each woman to describe honestly recent behavior of hers that fits any of the rungs on the Anger Ladder. Ask her to evaluate where her anger-handling behavior falls.

Give women time to write; then congratulate them on their work. Point out that although level 6 of anger-handling, "pleasant and rationally directed toward cause of anger," may *sound* easy, it can be very difficult.

ACTIVITY 3 – EXPRESSING ANGER (20 minutes)

Because "pleasantly and rationally" directing our anger toward its cause can be so hard, *Almost 13* describes a formula for doing it. This formula involves avoiding "you-messages" and using "I-messages" instead.

Review with women the "I-message"/"you-message" idea, originally developed by Dr. Thomas Gordon in his book, *Parent Effectiveness Training*.[6] Gordon says that a "you-message" is a statement of blaming, shaming, warning, or ordering. Its hallmark is that it contains the word *you*:

You stop that.
You should know better.
You are acting like a baby.
You slob.
If *you* don't stop that, then...

By contrast, an "I-message" describes how *I feel* when such and such is happening:

I cannot rest when someone is playing loud music.
I'm worried about getting dinner ready on time.
I get discouraged when I see my clean kitchen dirty again.
I get scared and worried that something awful has happened when it's after curfew and you're not in.

Note that most of these "I-messages" are not strictly expressions of anger! "I am convinced that anger is something generated solely by the parent *after* he has experienced an earlier feeling," says Gordon. "The parent manufactures the anger as a consequence of experiencing a primary feeling." [7]Examples are fear over a preteen's being late coming home, disappointment over a preteen's poor report card, embarrassment over a preteen's outlandish dress, fear that a preteen will behave immorally.

Ask women now to do the following work:

1. List three you-messages you recently sent to your preteen.
2. Identify the primary emotion behind each. (Was it really anger?)
3. Rewrite each you-message as an I-message.

When the women are finished, ask them to divide into

groups of three and share their rewritten "I-messages" with each other. The women will want to help keep each other honest and make sure there are no hidden "you-messages," even though it begins with the words "I feel."

ACTIVITY 4—SAYING NO (20 minutes)

Point out that saying no or giving a reprimand is rough because it means being assertive and taking an unpopular stand. It also means making someone else feel bad. Again, this experience is extremely unpleasant for those of us who have been schooled always to make others feel good. It may be so unpleasant in fact, that we may not even have the words to use to make a reprimand!

In their book *The One Minute Manager*, Kenneth Blanchard and Spencer Johnson describe what they call the One Minute Reprimand, which mothers as managers of their children might do well to heed.

Blanchard and Johnson say that "the One Minute Reprimand works well when you tell people *beforehand* that you are going to let them know how they are doing and in no uncertain terms."[8]

The first half of the reprimand consists of:

- reprimanding people immediately after the misdeed is discovered.
- telling people specifically what they did.
- telling people how you feel about what they did wrong.
- pausing for a few seconds to let them feel how you feel.

The second half of the reprimand consists of:

- touching them in a way that lets them know you are honestly on their side.
- reminding them how much you value them.
- reaffirming that you think well of them but not of their performance in this situation.
- realizing that when the reprimand is over, it's over.

Briefly discuss:
- How effective do you think that One Minute Reprimand might be with a preteen? Why?
- What other tips for reprimanding or saying no can you share from *Almost 13* or your own experience?

Now divide the women into groups of four to role-play saying no and reprimanding. Remind them to use "I-messages," and to follow the first *and* second parts of the One Minute Reprimand.

Close by thanking our Heavenly Parent, who always disciplines us honestly, wisely and lovingly.

Homework: Exercises 6 and 7 in chapter 7, "Good Housekeeping or Groady to the Max."

Week 7: Minoring on the Minors

Based on book chapter 7

> *Goals:* To give women a standard for use in distinguishing minor areas from major ones. To identify that which is merely "cultural."

Content summary: Many of the "changes" that appear in teens and preteens are merely "cosmetic" or cultural. Parents would do well to distinguish these minor matters from major value shifts.

You'll need: Old high school yearbooks and/or pictures and magazines from moms' teen era, contemporary teen magazines, worksheets from chapter 7, "Good Housekeeping or Groady to the Max."

ACTIVITY 1 – STORY SHARING (15 minutes)

Divide the women into groups of four for story-sharing. Ask each to tell two stories from her own early teen years: a time she and her parents had a major argument over a minor matter, and a time her parents handled a minor matter in an appropriately low-key manner.

ACTIVITY 2 – DRAWING THE LINE (15 minutes)

Based on the story-sharing you have just done, discuss:
• What, in your opinion, are some criteria for distinguishing a major area from a minor one?

Let women brainstorm. To sum up, suggest that as *Almost 13* points out, if it's a *moral* issue, it's a major. Anything else is minor.

Discuss:
• What are the dangers of majoring on the minors?

Point out that in their book, *Five Cries of Parents*, Merton and Irene Strommen give a simple acrostic to help parents remember the primary goals of adolescence. These are seven goals an adolescent intuitively seeks to achieve during the teen years.[9] The acrostic spells "*affirms*":

1. *Achievement*. The satisfaction of arriving at excellence in some area of endeavor.
2. *Friends*. The broadening of one's social base by learning to make friends and maintain them.
3. *Feelings*. The self-understanding gained by learning to share one's feelings with another person.
4. *Identity*. The sense of knowing "who I am," of being recognized as a significant person.
5. *Responsibility*. The confidence of knowing "I can stand alone and make responsible decisions."
6. *Maturity*. The transformation from a child into an adult.
7. *Sexuality*. The acceptance of responsibility for one's sexuality.

Discuss:
• How can giving preteens more latitude in the minor areas help them begin to achieve these goals of adolescence (particularly 4, 5, and 6)?

ACTIVITY 3 – COMPARE THE CULTURES (15 minutes)

Point out that often much of parents' distaste for their preteens' ways is simply a matter of *cultural difference*.

On one side of the room, post and/or display items from the moms' teen era: old yearbooks, pictures, clothes, and memorabilia. On the other side of the room, post and/or display items from current teen culture: record jackets, magazines, and clothes.

Ask women to form groups of eight and discuss:

* What was the cultural "norm" for your teen years?
* What is the current teen cultural "norm"?
* What is the current adult "norm"? What are the areas of conflict between teen standards and adult ones?
* How much of today's dress and music is purely cultural?
* Where does culture end and questions of morality begin to impinge?

ACTIVITY 4 – REDUCING MINOR FRICTION (15 minutes)

Ask women to share their worksheets, "Dealing with the Minors," with each other in the same groups of eight. They should focus particularly on helping each other brainstorm ways to reduce friction in the minor areas of tension.

Close by thanking the God whose love transcends all cultures.

Week 8: Majoring on the Majors

Based on book chapter 8

> *Goals:* To help parents define their own key moral values—the ones they hope to instill in their preteens. To give parents help in dealing with problem situations when preteens violate those values.

Content summary: Most parents have in mind a number of positive qualities and behaviors that they hope the preteen will choose to value and enact. It helps, however, for parents to have these, their cherished values, clearly in mind. Then they are better able to communicate them clearly and to deal with infractions of these values should they occur.

You'll need: Paper and pencil, large sheet of butcher paper, copies of professional people resource list (see activity 4).

NOTE: Consider making this meeting a fathers' invitational. The work of focusing on the major parental values can really only be done by BOTH parents as a team. A second-best choice would be to have the mothers do these activities first, then involve the fathers at a later time. But you may even wish to reschedule the time of this meeting in order to involve the fathers directly.

ACTIVITY 1 – KNOW YOUR OWN STAND (15 minutes)

Put the following thoughts into your own words:
Many groups, books, and codes give lists of desirable, positive, human qualities. Sometimes called "virtues" or "values," these lists are found in places as diverse as the Boy Scout code of honor to the fruits of the Spirit given in Galatians 5. What are some of the most important moral values, behaviors, and beliefs you have tried to instill in your preteen and hope he or she will choose to claim?

Give parents paper and pencil and ask them to list these virtues. Note that husband and wife should *not* consult with each other yet.

Now post a large sheet of paper and ask the group to share quickly their lists of values.

The group's list of virtues, behaviors, and values might include some or all of the following:
- truthful
- forgiving

- kind
- sexually pure
- self-accepting
- hard-working
- having strong faith in Christ
- courageous
- independent
- self-controlled

Again, have each participant go through his/her own list and the group list and rank the top five virtues they hope to see enacted by their preteen.

Now, have husband and wife compare notes. Do their key values differ? Where? Why? (If husbands are not present, wives should go through this exercise with them later.)

ACTIVITY 2—CREATE A CONTINUUM (15 minutes)

If husbands are present, they and their wives should choose their top three values and do the following activity.

If husbands are *not* present, have women choose their top three values, then get together in small groups of four to do this activity.

For each value or virtue, describe behavior on a continuum. At the far left of the continuum is positive behavior that exemplifies the virtue. At the far right is negative behavior that defies the virtue.

A continuum for truthfulness, for example, might look like this:

Tells truth even at cost to self.	Tells truth if no cost to self.	Tells occasional white lies.	Tells lies.	Cannot be depended on to tell truth.

After couples or groups have created their continuums, have each individual define the limits of behavior he or she considers acceptable in the preteen. He or she should mark each of the behaviors with one of the following numbers:

1. I can tolerate this behavior.
2. I prefer not to tolerate this behavior.
3. I will not tolerate this behavior.

Again, allow couples (or groups) to compare notes and discuss similarities and differences in their rankings.

ACTIVITY 3 – FREEDOM TO CHOOSE (10 minutes)

Share the following in your own words with the group:

"As adults, our responsibility is to set standards and demonstrate values," says Dr. Haim Ginott, wise and loving parent and author of *Between Parent and Teenager*. "[But] no one can mature by blindly obeying his parents."[10] We can and should set standards and limits, but in the end, the preteen herself must freely choose the value or virtue for herself. As *Almost 13* points out, a young person's "habit of conforming to your standards" is not the same as his taking mature responsibility for his own moral decisions.

Almost 13 gives a good example of leaving that responsibility for his own life with the teen, while still setting clear parental expectations. In the story of Jarrett and the keys, Dave asks Jarrett, "What do you think the next step is, Jarrett?" By this question, Dave is giving Jarrett the opportunity to be responsible for making his own moral choice.

Unfortunately, in the interests of enforcing their code of behavior, parents sometimes unwittingly take away their children's responsibility for their own lives. They coerce the children into "right" behavior, which ultimately backfires.

Now have the group break into fours (two couples or four women) for story-sharing. Each person should quickly share two stories:

• A time his/her parents used coercive measures to enforce right

• A time his/her parents gave clear guidelines, but left the responsibility of moral choice to the individual

ACTIVITY 4 – DEALING WITH PROBLEM SITUATIONS (20 minutes)

Ask the groups to remain in their foursomes, and use the remainder of the time to analyze and role-play solutions to problem situations.

Have each couple or individual present an actual problem situation that they are currently facing in a major value area with their preteen. The group should analyze the situation. Is the problem one of:

• no clear parental limits?

• heading off potential trouble at the pass? (Ex: faith beginning to waver, or bad peer influences beginning to creep in)

• dealing with actual disruptive behavior? (sneaking out at night, abuse of drugs, etc.)

Use the parents' own "I cannot tolerate" continuum, plus group concensus to determine the seriousness of the problem. Use group brainstorming and role play to suggest ways to deal with it. For example, the group may help a mother role-play how to confront a daughter whom she has discovered to be lying.

Spend the last several minutes of the time discussing when to seek professional help. Encourage parents not to be embarrassed or wait until the situation has reached a crisis before they seek help. Make available a list of professionals in your area, preferably Christian, to whom parents may turn for help if they need it. Include therapists, doctors, nurses, or clinics, any resident theologians, chapters of SADD (Students Against Drunk Driving), and contact persons for local Christian youth organizations such as Campus Life, Student Venture, and Young Life. At the top of the list will be your own pastor's name, the first person most parents will turn to in time of crisis.

Week 9: Teen Challenge, Teen Passage

Based on book Chapter 9

    Goals: To help women assist their teens in setting goals. To help women begin to set some of their own goals for growth.

    Content summary: A sense of achievement is a critical adolescent need. Parents can help teens gain that much-needed sense of achievement by assisting them in realistic goal-setting. But adults, too, need a sense of achievement, and can model growth for their teens by setting and working toward their own goals.

    You'll need: Copy of *Almost 13*, particularly exercise 8, "Steps to Develop a Teenage Challenge," for each participant, pencils, and paper. Women also need to bring their worksheets from chapter 2, the assessment of their teen's and their own strengths and weaknesses, based on the four personality types.

ACTIVITY 1 – A "RITE OF PASSAGE" (15 minutes)

Explain that, if we stop to think about it, all of our major life transitions or "passages" are marked by a celebration or ceremony. We have a marriage ceremony and reception to mark the passage of wedding. We have baby showers and family get-togethers to mark a baby's arrival into the world. We celebrate birthdays, graduations, anniversaries—all the other major life passages, even including death (though solemnly).

But what about the passage from childhood to adulthood? Most ancient societies, and many primitive ones today, have some celebration, often including a test of endurance, called a *rite of passage*. Think for instance of the Bar Mitzvah or Bat Mitzvah of Judaism, or of the rigorous solo ordeals of the youth of primitive tribes, or even of adolescent confirmation. All these ceremonies are a way of marking the child's transition into a new stage. They are a way of meeting the need for achievement, and of saying, "Yes, we now recognize you as a young adult. You are no longer a child."

Ask women to break into groups of four for story-sharing. Each woman should share a story of her adolescent "rite of passage." What event, achievement, or celebration in her life caused her to think, "Yes, now I'm really growing up!"

After the women have shared, discuss briefly:

• What is the advantage for adults of positively recognizing the young person's transition to young adulthood?

• What are the benefits of having the young person meet a series of goals or achievements?

ACTIVITY 2—MEASURABLE GOALS (10 minutes)

Explain that the "Teenage Challenge" described in chapter 9 of *Almost 13* is just such a beneficial "rite of passage." By challenging the preteen to new growth, it provides a much needed sense of accomplishment. And the whole process and succeeding celebration upon completion serve as a concrete, public marker of the preteen's new status. A preteen thus recognized by his/her parents will have much less need to "prove" his/her "adulthood" in negative ways!

Ask women to turn to chapter 9 of *Almost 13* and read the four points under number 5 of the "Steps to Develop a Teenage Challenge." These guidelines describe what constitutes a *measurable* goal: something *specific* and *achievable*.

Ask women to turn to page *143* and read aloud a few of the most measurable goals from the "Teenage Challenge for Jonathan." Now ask everyone to rewrite those same goals so they are not measurable—so they are vague and unattainable. For example, IV. A. might be rewritten thus: "Earn some money yourself." (Doesn't say, "How much?" "By when?")

Have a few of these "bad examples" read aloud. Have a good laugh.

ACTIVITY 3 – TEENAGE CHALLENGE (15 minutes)

Now ask the women to work individually on exercise 8, "Steps to Develop a Teenage Challenge," numbers IV, V, and VI. Women will need to refer back to their project from chapter 2, the teens' strengths and weaknesses.

After women have had time to work, ask them to share some of their goals. Have the group comment. Do the goals meet the checklist described in point VI?

Discuss briefly: How can we best arrive at concensus between our ideas and our teens' ideas? How can we make sure this Teenage Challenge is really *their* challenge—not ours?

ACTIVITY 4 – MOMS' CHALLENGE (20 minutes)

Point out that any mother who has a teenager is about to go through her own passage! Why not celebrate your own "rite of passage" by creating your own "Mom's Challenge"? Base it on the worksheet you did on yourself in week 2, and model it after the "Teenage Challenge," with goals for the physical, intellectual, spiritual, and practical areas.

Discuss briefly:

• What would be the advantages of your doing your own challenge at the same time your teenager is doing his or hers?

Possible benefits are as follows:

• helping mothers grow.

• giving mothers something of their own to work on so they are not tempted to "take over" their child's Teenage Challenge.

• making the mothers equal partners with the preteen, so the mothers can model achievement.

• helping the mothers celebrate their own passage.

Give the women the rest of the time to work on their own challenges. They may work in pairs if they wish, with a friend with whom they may share a mutual accountability.

Close by thanking God for every season of our lives, and the transitions and celebrations that mark their changes.

Week 10: The Path to Independence

Based on book chapter 10

> *Goals*: To help parents learn to "release" their children to independence.
>
> To help parents adjust to their own "new identity" as parents of a young person.

Content summary: The goal of parenthood is to work oneself out of a job. It's an old adage, but true: parents' objective is to bring their teens gradually to complete independence, which involves adjustment for both parties.

You'll need: Copies of project sheet, "Birthday Boxes," for each participant, copies of *Almost 13* for each participant (or each couple), paper, and pencil.

NOTE: Again, you may wish to make this a fathers' invitational. Creating a structure of growing independence for their teen merits the involvement of both parents, as does anticipating and planning for how that change will affect their own lives.

ACTIVITY 1 – DECISION-MAKING (20 minutes)

Put the following into your own words:

Author, lecturer, and parent Dr. Haim Ginott gives the following definition of maturity in *Between Parent and Teenager*: "An adult does not shift responsibility onto his parents. He shoulders his own burdens. He makes decisions and accepts the consequences. He endures anxiety, copes with guilt, and guides his conduct. Without such growing pains, there is no growth.... To become an adult, a teenager must go through the emotions, not just the motions, of adulthood."[11]

At the end of chapter 10, Claudia Arp, the author of *Almost 13,* gives us a plan for helping teens develop the decision-making skills that characterize a mature, responsible adult.

Review the decision-making steps briefly (beginning on page *163*), focusing especially on the negotiating skills of step 4 with its listing and ranking of pros and cons.

Now have the group break into teams of four (two couples, or four individuals if fathers aren't present). Ask each person or couple to think of a decision their teen is facing right now. Have them role-play the situation the "wrong" way—harassing the teen, taking his responsibility for making the decision away from him, and the "right" way—assisting the teen in developing decision-making skills through making this decision.

Debrief the role plays.

• To the people who played the teen: How did it feel to have your "parents" take the decision away from you? Leave it with you?

• To the people who played the parents: How did you feel taking charge of your "teen's" decision for him? Leaving it with him?

• What did you learn from these role plays that you could apply to real life?

ACTIVITY 2—GROWING INDEPENDENT TEENS (20 minutes)

Have parents now work on the project for this chapter, "Birthday Boxes." This is a big project! Even people who've already started it will doubtless want more time to refine it.

You may want couples to work on it alone if they're just beginning this project, or they may want to team up with other couples to polish off forgotten areas.

Allow some time for every couple to team up with another couple for about five minutes, to compare notes, and to help each other answer question 4: Am I releasing too much or not enough freedom to my teen? Am I giving my teen too much or not enough responsibility? Also have them answer a corollary question: Am I providing an even balance of freedom and responsibility?

ACTIVITY 3—GROWING INDEPENDENT PARENTS (20 minutes)

Point out that as the young person moves closer toward her "new identity" of young adulthood, the parents also move toward a new identity. No longer are they the parents of a dependent child, upon whom they must lavish loads of time and attention. Gradually, the parents—especially, perhaps, the mother—will find themselves less and less "needed," with more and more time on their hands.

Suggest that parents may want to make their own "Birthday Boxes" to outline their own moves toward increasing independence from their teen. What will they do with their time, energy, and talents? As one mother, who successfully and smoothly made the transition to her new identity put it, "If you could have your choice, what would you like to do?" Answering this question could well be the biggest challenge of all.

Allow parents the remainder of the time to work on their own projects. Then close by thanking God for making us each the unique individuals we are, with the opportunity to become all we can be.

Week 11: Trust

Based on book chapter 11

> *Goals*: To help women build trust in their relationship with their preteen.
> To help women build trust in their relationship with God.

Content summary: Trust is such a delicate commodity. Like an Alpine flower, it can be easily damaged and take a long time to grow again. But the good news is that it can grow again. Through God's help and healing, trust that has been hurt—even trust in Him—can be healed and restored.

You'll need: Copies of *Almost 13* for each participant, paper, and pencils.

ACTIVITY 1—WHERE DID TRUST GO WRONG? (15 minutes)

Begin by sharing in your own words the message of hope found in the content summary above. There is hope and healing from broken trust in broken relationships. But in order to be healed, we need to follow the prescription of James 5:16: "Confess your trespasses to one another and pray for one another that you may be healed." Remind women of the types of trust breakdown that can occur: those described in chapter 11 of *Almost 13* (the list that begins with "one mistake blocks any future trust").

Ask women to consider two areas:

1. Where did any of these trust breakdowns occur with me and my parents? How was the trust re-established?

2. Where have any of these trust breakdowns occurred with me and my teen?

Then have women break into twos for story-sharing—confession. After a woman shares a story about herself and her parents, her partner should pray for any healing that is still needed in that situation. After a woman shares a story about herself and her preteen, the partner should again pray for healing of the relationship.

Encourage women to maintain a quiet, worshipful air of confession, repentance, and healing throughout this activity.

ACTIVITY 2—HOW CAN TRUST BE REBUILT? (20 minutes)

Take a few minutes to review principles from this chapter—and from the entire book—about practical ways to rebuild trust in a relationship. Some principles from this chapter include offering new opportunities for trust, getting all the facts before making a judgment, not attacking, and forgiving and forgetting. Your group may also want to review material from chapters 3 and 6 about forgiveness, chapter 5 about listening, or chapter 8 about setting clear value limits (or other material from other chapters that is appropriate to your group).

Ask women to break into groups of four to help each other role-play practical solutions to problems of broken trust. Encourage women, if possible, to use actual situations they are facing. They may need to practice showing forgiveness, expressing disapproval, or giving praise. Your role players will of course adapt their behavior to the situation.

Be sure to use role reversal here, too—with the woman whose "problem" is being role-played taking the part of the preteen, while another woman plays the part of the mother.

Debrief the role plays using questions such as these:

• What did you learn from the role plays about being trusted? About trusting?

• Why is trust sometimes so painful?

• Does Jesus' injunction to be "wise as serpents and harmless as doves" have any bearing on our trust relationship with our preteens? If so, what?

ACTIVITY 3—MY TRUST IN GOD (15 minutes)

Point out that our trust in God—or lack of it—can profoundly affect all our trust relationships for good or for ill. Sometimes, without even being aware of it, we may have become suspicious of God because we feel He has "let us down."

Ask women to be quiet and prayerfully assess their own trust relationship with God right now. Ask them to consider these three questions. Each individual may wish to jot down her thoughts, or just think them.

1. On a scale of 1 to 10, with 10 being complete trust, how would I rank my present level of trust in God?

2. Can I point to any event—recent or long ago—that shook my trust in God? Where I felt He had let me down?

3. How can I re-establish, or grow, in my trust in God?

Toward the end of the contemplation, you may wish to invite any who have never initially put their trust in Christ to do so now. You may want to invite participants to put their names into John 3:16, as *Almost 13* suggests doing on page 173. Or, you may want to present the good news of salvation through your own words, or through some simple formulation such as "The Four Spiritual Laws." While you may or may not want to have those who wish to accept Christ raise their hands, do make it known that you'll be available to talk further after the meeting.

ACTIVITY 4—LETTING GO AND LETTING GOD (10 minutes)

Point out that releasing our child to God's care is perhaps one of the most important steps we can take as mothers.

Invite women to join you now in this releasing ceremony. Point out that this may be very scary, and that no one is under duress to join in. But if they are willing, it could be a powerful and freeing experience.

Have women pray aloud the italicized prayer after you, and follow the motion instructions in parentheses.

O Loving Heavenly Parent,

I thank You that You hold us with open hands (open hands, palms upward).

And I thank You that You hold our children the same way.

As the Apostle Paul said, "I am persuaded that neither death nor life, nor angels nor principalities nor powers, nor things present nor things to come, nor height nor depth, nor any other created thing, shall be able to separate us from the love of God that is in Christ Jesus our Lord."

This is Your Word, and I trust You.

You gave me my child to care for and nurture, and I have

held him/her close to my heart. (Clench fists tightly and cross arms over chest.)

Now, I am giving him/her back to You, as Hannah did with Samuel. (Slowly, unclench fists and open up arms, till arms are extended with palms up.)

I entrust him/her to Your tender care, knowing that all Your children are exceedingly precious to You.

Amen.

Encourage women to leave in silence and prayerfulness. Be aware of any who may wish to talk further with you about making a commitment to Christ.

If you or your group is uncomfortable with hand motions, try another option. Ask your mothers to write a prayer in which they release their child to God. You could offer direction by suggesting what might be included in their prayer (perhaps using the previous prayer as a model). They may keep the prayer or choose to tear it up as a further symbol of releasing their teen.

Week 12: Relax

Based on book chapter 12

> *Goals:* To help women learn to relax in their role as mothers.
>
> To give women an opportunity to review the "course."

Content summary: As women learn to "release" their teen to God's ultimate care, and as the teen grows in independence, women will find new areas of personal growth opening up for them.

You'll need: Paper and pencils, participants' own "Birthday Box" ideas from week 10, materials for "interest centers" (see activity 2,) copy of "Moms' Support Group Evaluation" for each participant (see activity 3).

ACTIVITY 1 – "I LOVE TO..." (15 minutes)

Point out to women that a whole new phase of their lives can be opening up now as they gain more time and energy for themselves. This session will again focus on planning and preparing for this new phase of life.

Ask women to break into groups of four for story-sharing. Each woman should share three "I love to" stories: "I love to work in my garden. Nothing gives me greater pleasure than to see plants blooming," or "I love to keep our household books. I love to organize and see all those neat rows of figures," and so on.

After a woman has shared, the other members of her foursome should give her feedback about how she might expand and diversify her "loves" now that she has more time. For instance, the woman who loves bookkeeping might offer her services to teach others how to do the same. Or, she might think of becoming a fulltime CPA. The woman who loves gardening might discover she loves helping people "bloom" just as much.

ACTIVITY 2 – INTEREST CENTERS (30 minutes)

This activity is really several rolled into one. Set up throughout your meeting area four "interest centers" to help women work on the four areas of growth suggested in chapter 12 of *Almost 13*. The four areas and suggested materials are listed below. Women may choose to spend all of the next thirty minutes at one center, or they may break up their time at several centers. Clearly label each center, provide a large table for writing space, and chairs. Write up the "project" on a large sheet of poster board or newsprint. Create the following centers:

1. Creative interest building
Project: Develop a plan to explore and/or expand your life interests.

Materials to place at center: Women's own "Birthday Boxes" from week 10, input from activity 1, life and career planning books (such as *What Color is Your Parachute,* by Richard Bolles), paper, pencils.

2. Marriage enrichment
Project: Develop a list of four "dates" that would be good for you and your partner. Make two all for fun, one for learning, and one for any other area you want to develop.
Materials to place at center: Entertainment sections of local magazines and newspapers, Yellow Pages or other lists of local organizations and activities, marriage enrichment books from library (including Claudia and Dave Arp's *Ten Dates for Mates* and their tape *Making Your Marriage Live,* Power Source), paper, pencils.

3. Time management
Project: Plan and organize your time to achieve a better balance of work, rest, play, relationship building, and any other areas important to you.
Materials to place at center: Hensley Grid from page 178 of *Almost 13*, other time management books from the library, paper, pencils.

4. Looking on the light side
Project: Find and clip or copy good jokes and cartoons that you enjoy and can share with your family. Laugh!
Materials to place at center: Books and magazines with good jokes and cartoons in them, like *Reader's Digest, The Wittenberg Door,* and *Saturday Evening Post.*

ACTIVITY 3 – MOMS' SUPPORT GROUP EVALUATION (15 minutes)

Hand out copies of the evaluation form on page 254 to women and give them about five minutes to complete it.
Then call for a time of informal sharing. Invite those who wish to share one "I learned" statement from their evaluations.

This can be a time of positive reinforcement and "battery charging" as the group comes to a close. Be sure to collect the evaluations from everyone.

Discuss how each Mom can be involved in forming new, "offshoot" Mom's Support Groups with other friends.

You may wish to end this meeting, and this Moms' Support Group, with a time of open prayer and praise, in which anyone is free to give her thanks to God for the group, for what she learned, for her preteen.

Moms' Support Group Evaluation

Please complete the following statements about your experience in this support group:

1. The biggest thing I learned was _____

_____

2. The best part of the group for me was _____

_____

3. The hardest part of the group for me was _____

_____

4. I could have done without _____

_____

5. Next time you run the group you might want to _____

_____

6. The impact this has had on me and my teen's relationship has been _____

_____

NOTES

Chapter 1
1. Scripture paraphrased from Psalm 103:11-12.
2. Dr. James Dobson, *Hide or Seek* (Old Tappan, N.J.: Fleming H. Revell Co., 1974), p. 99.

Chapter 2
1. Tim LaHaye, *Understanding the Male Temperament* (Old Tappan, N.J.: Fleming H. Revell Co., 1977), p. 56.
2. Merton and Irene Strommen, *Five Cries of Parents* (New York: Harper & Row, 1985), p. 6.
3. *Ibid.*, p. 33.

Chapter 3
1. Dr. Kevin Leman, *Smart Girls Don't* (Ventura, Calif.: Regal Books, 1982), p. 50.

Chapter 4
1. Jay Kesler, *Parents and Teenagers* (Wheaton, Ill.: Victor Books, 1984) p. 157.
2. Letter adapted from Helen Botel, *Parents' Survival Kit* (Garden City, New York: Doubleday and Company, Inc., 1979), p. 21.
3. Charles Swindoll, *Home, Where Life Makes Up Its Mind* (Portland, Oregon: Multnomah Press, 1980), p. 51.
4. Kesler, *Parents and Teenagers* (Wheaton, Ill.: Victor Books, 1984), p. 285.

Chapter 5
1. Bottel, *Parents' Survival Kit*, p. 42.
2. Strommen and Strommen, *Five Cries of Parents*, p. 75.
3. *Ibid.*, p. 76.
4. *Ibid.*

Chapter 6
1. Dr. Haim Ginott, *Between Parent and Teenager* (New York: The Macmillan Company, 1969), p. 89.
2. "Into the Mouths of Babes," *Time Magazine*, July 15, 1985, p. 68.
3. *Ibid.*
4. *Ibid.*
5. Adapted from Dr. Ross Campbell, *How to Really Love Your Teenager* (Wheaton, Ill.: Victor Books, 1981), pp. 66-69.
6. *Ibid.*, p. 68.
7. *Ibid.*
8. Adapted from Ginott's *Parent and Teenager*, p. 89.

Chapter 8
1. Dr. Bruce Narramore, *Adolescence Is Not an Illness* (Old Tappan, N.J.: Fleming H. Revell, Co., 1980), p. 32.

Notes

2. Art Linkletter and George Gallup, Jr., *My Child on Drugs? Youth and the Drug Culture* (Cincinnati, Ohio: Standard Publishing Company, 1981), p. 15.

3. *Ibid.*

4. "The Chemistry of Craving," *Psychology Today*, October 1983, pp. 37-38.

5. Linkletter and Gallup, pp. 84-85.

6. Narramore, pp. 66-67.

7. Susan Schaeffer Macaulay, *How To Be Your Own Selfish Pig* (Elgin, Illinois: Chariot Books, 1982), p. 17.

Chapter 9

1. Kesler, *Parents and Teenagers*, p. 356.

Chapter 10

1. Ken Poure, *Parents: Give Your Kid a Chance* (Irvine, California: Harvest House Publishers, 1977), adapted from pp. 83-93.

Chapter 11

1. Fritz Ridenour, *What Teenagers Wish Their Parents Knew About Kids* (Waco, Texas: Word Publishers, 1982), p. 172.

2. Strommen and Strommen, *Five Cries of Parents*, p. 97, 98.

3. Ridenour, *What Teenagers Wish Their Parents Knew About Kids*, p. 178

Chapter 12

1. Pat Baker, *Help, I've Just Given Birth to a Teenager* (Grand Rapids, Mich.: Baker Book House, 1981), p. 73.

Chapter 14

1. Quoted in Jay Kesler's *Parents and Teenagers*, p. 157.

2. Strommen and Strommen, *Five Cries of Parents*, p. 14.

3. Roland and Doris Larson, *I Need to Have You Know Me* (Minneapolis: Winston Press, 1979), pp. 35-36.

4. Strommen and Strommen, *Five Cries of Parents*, p. 64.

5. Barbara Varenhorst, *Real Friends: Becoming the Friend You'd Like to Have* (San Francisco: Harper & Row, 1984), p. 58.

6. Dr. Thomas Gordon, *Parent Effectiveness Training* (New York: Plume Books, 1970), pp. 115, 123.

7. *Ibid.*, p. 126.

8. Kenneth Blanchard, Ph.D., and Spencer Johnson, M.D., *The One Minute Manager* (New York: Berkley Books, 1981), p. 59.

9. Strommen and Strommen, *Five Cries of Parents*, p. 33.

10. Dr. Haim G. Ginott, *Between Parent and Teenager* (New York: Avon Books, 1969), p. 150.

11. *Ibid.*, p. 176.